The Complete Guide to Growing Tomatoes:

Everything You Need to Know Explained Simply —

Including Heirloom Tomatoes

by Cherie H. Everhart

Foreword by Don Rosenberg
www.InstantOrganicGarden.com

THE COMPLETE GUIDE TO GROWING TOMATOES: EVERYTHING YOU NEED TO KNOW EXPLAINED SIMPLY — INCLUDING HEIRLOOM TOMATOES

Library of Congress Cataloging-in-Publication Data

Everhart, Cherie H.
  The complete guide to growing tomatoes : everything you need to know explained simply - including heirloom tomatoes / by Cherie H. Everhart.
     p. cm.
  Includes bibliographical references and index.
  ISBN-13: 978-1-60138-350-1 (alk. paper)
  ISBN-10: 1-60138-350-9 (alk. paper)
  1. Tomatoes. 2. Tomatoes--Varieties. I. Title.
  SB349.E94 2010
  635'.642--dc22
                              2010008305

Printed in the United States

PROJECT MANAGER: Kimberly Fulscher • PEER REVIEWER: Marilee Griffin • ASSISTANT EDITOR: Holly Marie Gibbs
ASSISTANT EDITOR: Amber McDonald • INTERIOR DESIGN: Holly Marie Gibbs • PRE-PRESS & PRODUCTION
DESIGN: Samantha Martin • FRONT COVER DESIGN: Meg Buchner • BACK COVER DESIGN: Jackie Miller

Printed on Recycled Paper

We recently lost our beloved pet "Bear," who was not only our best and dearest friend but also the "Vice President of Sunshine" here at Atlantic Publishing. He did not receive a salary but worked tirelessly 24 hours a day to please his parents. Bear was a rescue dog that turned around and showered myself, my wife, Sherri, his grandparents Jean, Bob, and Nancy, and every person and animal he met (maybe not rabbits) with friendship and love. He made a lot of people smile every day.

We wanted you to know that a portion of the profits of this book will be donated to The Humane Society of the United States. *–Douglas & Sherri Brown*

The human-animal bond is as old as human history. We cherish our animal companions for their unconditional affection and acceptance. We feel a thrill when we glimpse wild creatures in their natural habitat or in our own backyard.

Unfortunately, the human-animal bond has at times been weakened. Humans have exploited some animal species to the point of extinction.

The Humane Society of the United States makes a difference in the lives of animals here at home and worldwide. The HSUS is dedicated to creating a world where our relationship with animals is guided by compassion. We seek a truly humane society in which animals are respected for their intrinsic value, and where the human-animal bond is strong.

Want to help animals? We have plenty of suggestions. Adopt a pet from a local shelter, join The Humane Society and be a part of our work to help companion animals and wildlife. You will be funding our educational, legislative, investigative and outreach projects in the U.S. and across the globe.

Or perhaps you'd like to make a memorial donation in honor of a pet, friend or relative? You can through our Kindred Spirits program. And if you'd like to contribute in a more structured way, our Planned Giving Office has suggestions about estate planning, annuities, and even gifts of stock that avoid capital gains taxes.

Maybe you have land that you would like to preserve as a lasting habitat for wildlife. Our Wildlife Land Trust can help you. Perhaps the land you want to share is a backyard—that's enough. Our Urban Wildlife Sanctuary Program will show you how to create a habitat for your wild neighbors.

So you see, it's easy to help animals. And The HSUS is here to help.

2100 L Street NW • Washington, DC 20037 • 202-452-1100
www.hsus.org

Dedication

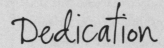

This book is dedicated to my dad, Harry Hart-man, who had a passion for everything out-side: hunting, fishing, wildlife, and vegetable gardening. He grew tomatoes (and other vegetables) almost all of his life. I continue to find it easy to conjure up an image of him with a saltshaker in his hand, eating freshly picked tomatoes like apples. I can't say that the love of gardening is always an inherited trait, but in this case, I think it was.

A special appreciation for my editor, Kim Fulscher, who made a rough manuscript much better, and for my youngest daughter, Erin, who encouraged me to attempt writing in the first place. It is a wonderful experience to learn from people who are young enough to be (or are) your children.

Trademark Statement

All trademarks, trade names, or logos mentioned or used are the property of their respective owners and are used only to directly describe the products being provided. Every effort has been made to properly capitalize, punctuate, identify, and attribute trademarks and trade names to their respective owners, including the use of ® and ™ wherever possible and practical. Atlantic Publishing Group, Inc. is not a partner, affiliate, or licensee with the holders of said trademarks.

Table of Contents

Chapter 8: Dealing With Pests and Disease   157

Chapter 9: Organic Tomato Gardening   185

Chapter 10: Heirloom Tomatoes   209

Chapter 11: Harvesting and Using
Your Tomato Crop   223

Foreword

There is nothing better than the taste of homegrown tomatoes. Tomatoes bought from mega-chain grocery stores do not even deserve the same name, but tomatoes at the organic food store are expensive, and the farmers' market is a long drive. Therefore, the best solution is to grow your own; however, many people don't know how to garden anymore.

Enter Cherie Everhart. If there is anything you ever wanted to know about tomatoes, it is in Everhart's *The Complete Guide to Growing Tomatoes: Everything You Need to Know Explained Simply — Including Heirloom Tomatoes*. Everything you ever wanted or needed to know about tomatoes is included in this book, from the history of the tomato, the botany behind gardening, how to prepare soil, and starting seeds and planting transplants — Everhart covers it all. This book will teach you about tomato care, different growing methods, harvesting, and even preserving. You will learn the stories behind some of the most popular heirloom varieties, from Abe Lincoln to Brandywine and Mr. Stripey.

The best part is that this book is great for beginners, but also full of tips for more experienced gardeners. For the gardening newcomer, you will learn the basics and take the mystery out of gardening because the techniques described here apply to gardening in general, not just tomatoes. Gardening experts will pick up valuable tips on how to grow better tomatoes as well as learn some of the science behind the techniques.

So, here begins your journey to growing the best tomatoes on the block.

Don Rosenberg

North Carolina Master Gardener
Author of *No Green Thumb Required! Organic Family
Gardening Made Easy*
Founder of Instant Organic Garden
www.InstantOrganicGarden.com

Introduction

Home vegetable gardens are sprouting up everywhere. Driven partly by the popularization of the local food movement, partly by continuing interest in organic gardening, and partly by demands of a tough economy, the popularity of gardens is growing. People who have never gardened before, and also those who gave it up years ago, are spending more of their time in the garden. Some have described this move as reminiscent of the victory gardens, which blossomed in World War I and II as a way for all to contribute to the war effort. Surveys by the National Gardening Association find that 43 million American families planted fruit or vegetable gardens in 2009, an increase of 19 percent from 2008. Even the First Family planted a vegetable garden at the White House in 2009. While family gardens have always been a staple of rural America, families in suburban and even urban areas are finding spots for gardens among the landscape shrubs and on decks, patios, and even apartment rooftops. Overwhelmingly, tomatoes are the most popular vegetable crop planted in the home garden. Tomatoes are grown in 86 percent of American home vegetable gardens, a testament to both the popularity of tomatoes in the American diet and to their abundant productivity in the garden.

Despite the fact that we have been growing tomatoes for generations, tomato-growing habits and practices are continuing to evolve and improve. Like many, I started my first tomato plot when I was a child, probably around 10 years old. My parents let me dig up the grass in a small spot in the backyard next to the fence. I was hooked and have had a garden ever since — with short breaks while I was a teenager and when I went to college. Even while living in apartment-style housing with very limited space, I never had a garden that did not include a few tomato plants. Since my first garden, I have expanded the space; added more varieties; included heirlooms in the mix; improved my support strategies; tried an endless array of tricks for deterring deer and other pests; and started a compost pile. I have had small gardens, big gardens, and container gardens. I have also eaten an uncountable number of tomato sandwiches, made lots of sauce, put up endless freezer bags of tomatoes, experimented with new salsa recipes, and given away armfuls of the extra bounty.

Over the last decade or so, one of the biggest changes in tomato growing has been the increased interest in the incorporation of organic gardening approaches. This change runs parallel to an increased interest generally in local produce and a broader interest in how and where our food is grown. Another change over the last decade is an increase in the knowledge of and interest in heirloom tomatoes. Heirloom vegetables are those varieties that have been cultivated and selected by gardeners over generations and sometimes over centuries. Seeds from these heirloom plants have been saved and passed down over time to preserve favorite or unique varieties. Home gardeners have discovered heirloom tomatoes, and local market growers have found that restaurants and farmers' market buyers have a new interest in heirlooms and a willingness to pay a premium over standard hybrid tomatoes. The interest in heirloom tomatoes is based in a desire to preserve older gardening traditions as well as in a willingness for broadening our culinary expectations beyond the red, round slicing tomato.

Overview of Book Content

Why, then, do you need to read a book on growing tomatoes? While the beginning gardener will surely get tomatoes from his or her first crop, a variety of factors in the garden can greatly influence the quality, ease, and abundance of the crop. Many of these factors are well within the control of the gardener. When you initially embark on tomato growing, you can either be oblivious to variables that have a big impact on your crop or you can be overwhelmed by the choices you must make. Choices about things like varieties to grow, sites, soil amendments, watering systems, fertilizer, and pest control can have a huge impact on both the quality and the abundance of your harvest. Furthermore, the typical home gardener does not grow only tomatoes. A meaningful side benefit of a focus on tomatoes and of learning the best techniques for optimizing the homegrown tomato crop is the opportunity to apply that learning to other crops in your garden. While the specific choices may differ depending on the vegetable, the variables and considerations will apply broadly to many other vegetables in the home garden. This book is written to educate home gardeners about growing, preserving, and eating tomatoes and to assist them in making choices in the abundance of variables, which they can adjust to assure the best tomato crop possible. This book will also further develop skills for growing other vegetables.

The objective of this book is to provide a detailed discussion of the ins and outs of preparing for and executing a great tomato garden. It starts with a discussion of how and why the tomato came to be such a large part of our gardening repertoire and our diet. It includes a chapter on organic gardening and how it applies to and benefits your tomato garden. It also includes a chapter on the increasingly popular heirloom tomato, describing what is different and special about these tomatoes and why they should be considered for your garden. Finally, it includes a broad description of the best ideas for harvesting, cooking, and preserving your tomato crop.

Popularity of Tomatoes

Why we eat tomatoes

Tomatoes are ubiquitous in the American diet due to their versatility in the kitchen, their ease of cultivation, their low cost, and the health benefits that they offer. Tomatoes can be found in every meal of the day, from a breakfast drink or favorite omelet ingredient, to a garnish on a lunch sandwich, to the primary component of a pasta sauce at dinner. They are found in fast food and in gourmet kitchens. They are regularly in dishes like salads, soups, pizzas, stews, pastas, omelets, and sandwiches. They can be eaten alone or tastefully combined with a variety of other vegetables.

Tomatoes can be prepared fully ripened or picked pre-ripe for unique specialty dishes. They are eaten raw, cooked, pickled, pureed, and dried. They are mixed with a variety of other vegetables, spices, cheeses, or breads to create cookbooks full of favorite dishes. Tomatoes find their way into beverages, both nonalcoholic and alcoholic, and are a component of some of our favorite condiments and dips.

The growth of the fast food industry has been a major boon for the commercial tomato farms, as tomatoes have become a standard component of the hamburger, the pizza, and the deli sandwich. Ketchup alone accounts for a good deal of American tomato consumption, with 97 percent of American homes containing bottles of the tomato-based condiment in the kitchen. We have become accustomed to seeing tomatoes in both the produce section of our grocery store and the canned vegetable aisle. Like many vegetables, fresh tomatoes are eaten year-round in the American diet, thanks to industrial growers in Florida, California, Mexico, and Canada. In the typical produce section, you are likely to find up to six different varieties of fresh tomatoes. In a walk down the canned food aisle, you will sometimes find a 12-food section devoted to tomatoes: stewed, chopped, minced, and prepared as sauces and pastes. Individuals trying to avoid tomatoes in their diets would have quite a challenge in current American culture.

All these factors have contributed to making tomatoes one of the most popular vegetables in the American diet, second only to the potato, in both farm value and in United States consumption. Granted, much of the tomato consumption in the United States is driven by the consumption of processed tomatoes in ketchup and sauces. Just considering fresh vegetables, the tomato is the fourth most popular fresh-market vegetable in the United States behind potatoes, lettuce, and onions. The average American eats roughly 90 pounds of fresh tomatoes and tomato products annually, according to the Heinz® Ketchup Company. While this number sounds pretty impressive, we are a good distance behind the world leaders in tomato consumption. The Greeks and the Libyans consume more than 200 pounds of tomato products per person per year. Consumption continues to grow, both for fresh tomatoes and for processed tomatoes, partly driven by the increased variety of tomatoes, the growth of the Latino population in the United States, and the surge in popularity of Mexican and pizza restaurants in the United States. The success of this food and its myriad array of processed products creates a farmed-tomato revenue of more than $2 billion in the United States.

Tomatoes are found internationally, in diets covering every continent. In some cuisines — Italian, Spanish, and Mexican, to name a few — it is hard to imagine preparing a classic meal without using the tomato. Thanks in part to the growth of the fast food industry around the world, tomatoes have spread to all parts of the world in sandwiches, salads, and ketchup. China has become the largest producer of tomatoes in the world, and while processed tomatoes do not figure prominently in the Chinese diet the way it does in the American diet, the Chinese consumed 40 pounds of fresh tomatoes per capita in 2008.

Why we grow tomatoes

Tomatoes are grown in home gardens in every state in the nation. While tomatoes prefer warmer weather, avid gardeners in colder climates go to great lengths to extend their growing seasons by starting plants inside and covering plants to protect them from early and late frosts. Gardeners in warm weather climates often leverage their warm locales and stretch the season to get multiple crops of tomatoes. Tomatoes targeted for commercial scale production and processing are grown in 20 states. The popular vegetable and fruit is relatively easy and cost effective to grow commercially. Tomatoes targeted for the winter and spring grocery market are grown primarily in Florida and Mexico. Over the years, they have been bred to be hardy, thick-skinned, and durable for shipping. So the crop is red and ripe when it gets on the grocery shelf, tomatoes can be picked green or light pink and are carefully managed during the shipping process to assure ripening throughout transit time. They are extremely productive, can be machine-harvested, and a single seed will easily produce a bushel of tomatoes. In 2009, California led the nation in growing ripe tomatoes targeted for the processed foods market. In the summer months, local farms, roadside stands, and backyard gardens gear up and some of the tomato production shifts to local vine-ripe versions.

Greenhouse tomatoes have become an increasingly important part of the fresh tomato market and are grown and targeted for grocery store produce sections. These tomatoes are grown in Canada, the United States, and Mexico, and include the popular on-vine or cluster tomatoes as well as beefsteak tomatoes. Consumers tend to like the brighter, deep red color of these varieties and find the smell of the attached vines appealing. Taste is subjective, but surprisingly, in some taste testing, no major taste differences have been found between the commercial field-grown and greenhouse-grown tomatoes.

While few home gardeners embark on a backyard vegetable garden with the primary objective of saving money, there is certainly the opportunity to do so. A successful tomato plant in a long season climate can produce up to a bushel (about 50 pounds) of tomatoes. Prices for tomatoes during the 2009 summer months across the United States averaged around $1.70 per pound. In theory, this translates to roughly $90 worth of tomatoes produced from a single plant. A single packet of seeds can easily produce hundreds of dollars worth of tomatoes, and a clever and energetic gardening family can consume and preserve the bulk of this harvest.

The difference is not easily missed between the taste of local, freshly grown tomatoes and tomatoes picked pre-ripe and shipped to grocery stores from Florida or Mexico. This difference in taste and texture is apparent to even the most casual of cooks and consumers and unmistakable to the dedicated tomato grower. The difference between homegrown and grocery store taste quality is probably more dramatic for tomatoes than for any other common vegetable. One would be hard pressed to identify this difference in taste tests for other common vegetables like carrots, lettuce, peppers, or potatoes. This surely accounts for a large part of the interest in growing homegrown tomatoes. Based on nutritional analyses, this difference is not just in taste and texture. Local vine-ripe tomatoes have shown in numerous studies to contain significantly more vitamins and key nutrients than those picked green and ripened in shipping.

Health benefits of tomatoes

Over the last few decades, there has been increased public awareness of the health benefits of fruits and vegetables in general and of tomatoes in particular. Several studies have indicated that reduced risks of some cancers and heart disease may be linked to diets consisting of higher proportions of tomatoes or tomato products. Several studies have looked at the connection between tomato consumption and cholesterol levels. In a study conducted at the University of Finland in 2007, a tomato-rich diet was linked to a decrease of 5.9 percent in total cholesterol and a reduction in LDL (low density lipoprotein) cholesterol of 12.9 percent. Based on this and other similar studies, in 2009 a biotechnology spin-off company from Cambridge University introduced a "one-a-day" nutritional supplement based on the natural antioxidant lycopene found in tomatoes. A variety of specific studies have been executed in both animals and humans. These studies are aimed at looking for connections between tomatoes and treating an extensive list of cancers, including prostate, colon, breast, and pancreatic cancer. Many have found encouraging links of tomato consumption to a reduced risk for these cancers. With respect to heart disease, a large study among women has found a 34 percent reduction in cardiovascular disease for those women who ate more than two servings of tomatoes weekly. This study is consistent with other work showing an association between some key vitamins and nutrients found in tomatoes and reduced cardiovascular disease.

Nutrition Facts

per serving
Serving Size: 1 C chopped or diced tomatoes, 180g

Amount per serving		% Daily Value
Calories	32.4	2%
Calories from Carbohydrates	25.5	1%
Calories from fat	3	0%
Calories from Protein	3.9	0%
Total Fat	0.4 g	0%
Saturated Fat	0.4 g	0%
Monounsaturated Fat	0.1 g	0%
Polyunsaturated Fat	0.1 g	0%
Total Omega-3 fatty acids	5.4 mg	0%
Total Omega-6 fatty acids	144 mg	0%
Sterols		
Cholesterol	0 mg	0%
Phytosterols	13 mg	0%
Protein	1.6 g	3%
Vitamins		
Vitamin A	1499 IU	30%
Vitamin C	22.9 mg	38%
Vitamin E	1.0 mg	5%
Vitamin K	14.2 mcg	18%
Thiamin	0.07 mg	4%
Riboflavin	0.03 mg	2%
Niacon	1.1 mg	5%
Vitamin B6	0.14 mg	7%
Folate	27.0 mcg	7%
Pantothenic Acid	0.16 mg	2%
Choline	12.1 mg	
Betaine	0.2 mg	
Minerals		
Calcium	18.0 mg	2%
Iron	0.49 mg	3%
Magnesium	20.0 mg	5%
Phosphorus	43.0 mg	4%
Potassium	427 mg	12%
Sodium	9.0 mg	0%
Zinc	0.31 mg	2%
Copper	0.11 mg	5%
Manganese	0.21 mg	10%

Percent values are based on a 2,000 calorie per day diet. Your daily values may differ.

Additional Information

Water	170.1 g

Reported in a 2006 study published in the *American Journal of Clinical Nutrition*, people eating tomato extract were found to have a lower risk of blood clots, an effect analogous to that offered by aspirin. A tomato a day keeps the doctor away.

As mentioned previously, tomatoes are a source of lycopene, which is in the same chemical class, the carotenoids, as beta-carotene and is responsible for the red color of the tomato. Lycopene is a powerful, naturally occurring antioxidant that helps protect cells from the degenerative effects of free radicals and various other environmental challenges. Lycopene has also been shown to improve the skin's ability to protect against potentially harmful ultraviolet rays. While other fruits and vegetables contain lycopene, no other vegetable contains it in the amounts found in tomatoes. Interestingly, the amount of lycopene in tomatoes increases with heat, so cooked tomatoes tend to carry a greater supply of this healthy plant chemical. Tomatoes also contain healthy amounts of vitamin C, potassium, fiber, and beta-carotene. The human body then converts beta-carotene to vitamin A, an essential nutrient that aids in clear vision, bone growth, tooth development, and reproduction.

Another component of tomatoes that has received some attention lately in the dietary health arena are flavonoids. Flavonoids are a class of water-soluble pigments that can have useful anti-oxidant and anti-inflammatory properties. In the tomato, they are located primarily in the skin, but there are small amounts in the meat of the fruit. Studies at BASF Chemical Company with mice have found a correlation between a reduction in cardiovascular disease risk and the consumption of tomatoes rich in flavonoids. Other studies have demonstrated the ability to genetically engineer tomato varieties with increased levels of these flavonoids.

There are thousands of varieties of tomato plants, and the nutritional compositions of tomatoes vary widely across varieties and with different growing conditions. In addition, there are some tomato varieties that have been specifically bred to increase particular nutritional components. As an example, the Double Rich tomato has been engineered to contain twice the typical amount of vitamin C as the average tomato plant. This actually translates to the vitamin C content of a typical orange. Another example of nutrition-focused breeding is the beta-carotene-rich tomatoes. These tomatoes contain up to 20 times the amount of beta-carotene as found in a typical tomato. They are identified by names referring to their genetic lines (97L63, 97L66, and 97L97) and are available through several specialty tomato seed vendors. Recognizing that nutritional content of tomatoes varies widely, the following summary of nutritional information is meant to be a general guide for the average garden-grown tomato.

Using this Book to Maximize Tomato Quality, Output, and Enjoyment

There is both promise and peril offered by the ease of growing tomatoes. Due to the productivity and resilience of the tomato plant, even the most uninformed and inattentive gardener can enjoy some excellent tomatoes if the weather, the insects, and the local wildlife are cooperative. This potential for some success often can discourage the tomato gardener from searching for resources to broaden, optimize, and expand his or her tomato production. However, weather, insects, and local wildlife do not always cooperate. Evidence is clear, both from academic and USDA research making the most of all the many variables affecting tomato production and harvest can have a huge benefit on ultimate success in quality and quantity.

I hope this book will introduce the new tomato gardener to, and remind the experienced tomato grower of, some of the key factors that influence and sometimes control the success of the tomato crop. While the most analytical and studious of readers will benefit greatly from applying the information from this book to their gardens, another factor can certainly be at work. While the book attempts to be comprehensive, there is also enormous variability in the local climate, soil, light, and general conditions for every garden. Conversation with local experts, extension agents, or knowledgeable folks at your community nurseries can be invaluable in fine-tuning practices to get the most with your local growing conditions. Furthermore, experimenting in your own garden is invaluable to discover the factors that will be most effective in maximizing the particular results that you are looking for. Finally, there is enormous value in treating each growing season as an actual experiment. Creating and maintaining a garden log can be invaluable in not only assisting your memory but in also allowing a more accurate look at the factors and variables affecting your tomato success. It is also a wonderful diary to record what are sure to be great memories of past harvests.

Chapter 1:

A Short History of Tomatoes

The First Tomatoes

Origins of the tomato

As befitting of one of our most popular vegetables, there continues to be controversy in the botanical and agricultural community regarding the origins of the tomato plant. One school of thought supports a South American origin and another supports a Mexican birthplace. This debate continues to be the source of ongoing research in the botanical community, but the bulk of evidence seems to support the wild tomato as being indigenous to South America. Wild tomato plants continue to grow in several coastal regions of Peru, Chile, and Ecuador. Wild tomatoes have also been found in the Galapagos Islands; many assume that the seeds were transported there in

the digestive system of sea turtles. Like the birthplace question, many continue to question the location of the first tomato plant domestication and its use in local cooking. It appears that the Mayans, and potentially other Central American peoples, were the first to domesticate the tomato and incorporate it into their diets. Sometime after, tomatoes reached the Aztecs and were readily incorporated into their diets. The Spanish who visited or lived in this area report that the Aztecs were combining tomatoes with chilies to make what was probably a precursor to salsa.

The domestic tomato made its way north, and by the 16th century it was likely cultivated in southern Mexico. The Spanish were responsible for beginning the spread of the tomato around the world. They introduced the tomato into the Caribbean and also into the Philippines, both of which were then part of the Spanish Empire. From the Philippines, it likely made its way into Asia.

Tomatoes in Europe and North America

Spanish distribution

The Spanish were responsible for bringing the first tomatoes to Europe, following the conquest of Mexico by Hernán Cortes in 1520. The Spanish had a global empire during this period and as a result, the tomato began its journey around the world. The Spanish first spread the tomato and some of its culinary dishes to many of the Spanish colonies in the Caribbean. The tomato also made its way to Asia, thanks to the Spanish who initially took it to the Philippines, which was then a Spanish colony. From the Philippines, the tomato eventually made its way into and through the Asian continent.

Because much of what we consider Italy was part of the Spanish empire at this time, the tomato quickly became popular in Italy. The first recorded description of the tomato as a plant was in 1544 in Italy. It was called a golden apple (*mala aurea*) and described as flattened, segmented, and golden in color when ripe. In the second edition of the tomato information published in 1554, the name was changed to the *pomi d'oro* (also translated as golden apple), which is a name that continues to be used in Italy today. In Italy, they were initially cultivated as curiosity or ornamental plants, and were sometimes used for medicinal purposes. It is possible that another early Italian name for the tomato was *poma amoris*, or "love apples," because they were once believed to be aphrodisiacs. It should be mentioned that many plants that were then considered exotic fruits and vegetables were considered aphrodisiacs. The romantic and poetic nature of the "love apple" name caught on and continued to be used in many circles to refer to the tomato as it spread throughout Europe. The climates of Italy and Spain were very compatible with the tomato, so it was easily cultivated in this area and its popularity in the Mediterranean diets began to grow. Many tomato recipes, both Italian and Spanish, have their roots in this general time period.

In the mid-1700s, scientists begin to debate the botanical classification of the tomato. It was initially placed in the genus Solanum and called the *Solanum lycopersicum*, with *lycopersicum* being identified as the species name. This name was derived from the Latin word for wolf-peach. Shortly after, the tomato was reclassified into the genus *lycopersicon* and this name was used for several centuries. Recent genetic evidence has shown that, in fact, the original classification of the tomato in the Solanum genus was correct. This puts it in the same genus as the eggplant and the chili pepper.

The tomato arrives in the United Kingdom

The tomato made its way north through Europe and arrived in Britain in the late 1500s. While there was knowledge of the success of the Spaniards and Italians in incorporating tomatoes into their diets, the initial reaction of the British was not very positive. It was already known that the tomato stem and foliage are poisonous and that some of the tomato's botanical relatives are also poisonous. The tomato contains a toxic alkaloid that affects the gastrointestinal system and the neurological system. The alkaloid tends to concentrate in the foliage and stem with only minute amounts found in the fruit. Due to this characteristic, a view developed in Britain that the tomato fruit was poisonous as well. While the plant was cultivated and shared for its ornamental properties and as a botanical curiosity, the idea that the tomato was poisonous persisted, and few in Britain were interested in incorporating it into their diets. Some were willing to acknowledge that Southern Europeans did eat the tomato, but characterized the tomato as a light, refreshing vegetable that might be tolerable in the warm climates of the Mediterranean.

To these people, the tomato was certainly not appropriate or healthy for the colder, and maybe more civilized, areas of Britain. However, numerous British individuals advocated for the medicinal properties of the tomato in applications as diverse as salves for burns and itches, treatments for headaches, or treatments for gout. Amazingly, this general view of the undesirability of the tomato as a food persisted in Britain for the next almost 200 years. In the mid 1700s, the bias and misconceptions about the tomato started to break down and some British began to add the tomato to their diet in small portions, probably starting first with immigrant populations that had made their way from Southern Europe. With this spark of interest, acceptance of the tomato caught on quickly. By the end of the 18th century, the tomato was in daily use in Britain in sauces, soups, and stews.

The tomato migrates to North America

The route of the tomato to North America had many branches. The Spaniards likely created the first path in the late 1500s or early 1600s, when they brought the tomato to Florida, Georgia, and South Carolina. Most major Spanish settlements were in the coastal areas of these states, so the tomato was adopted much earlier in these areas than in the interior areas of these states. Like the Mediterranean, the Southeast region had a warm climate with a long growing season that was conducive to the success of the cultivation of the tomato. In these areas, the tomato was not compromised by stories and conceptions about its poisonous properties, so settlers here were much more willing and open to experimenting with both growing and incorporating it into their diets. Another route to North America probably came from the Caribbean via immigration into Florida, or as a result of the slave trade between the Caribbean islands and the United States. The native islanders, like the Spaniards, were assumably already avid tomato fans and naturally brought with them this tomato enthusiasm.

The first written reference to the tomato is from 1710 by herbalist William Salmon, who reported seeing tomatoes in what is now South Carolina. By the mid-1700s, people cultivated tomatoes on plantations and large farms in the Carolinas. Thomas Jefferson is also a key figure in the history of the tomato in the United States. Jefferson was an avid gardener who supported and encouraged the cultivation of a variety of plants and vegetables at his plantation in Monticello, Virginia. He wrote notes on growing and using tomatoes in the late 1700s, and could have been responsible for bringing some specific varieties over from France.

An additional path into the American colonies was from Britain. In this case, travelers, visitors, and settling colonists from the United Kingdom, carried these seeds as part of their move to the new world. Seeds carried by these groups, reached almost every settlement region of the developing American colonies. Seeds arriving from Britain also carried with them some of the same prejudices and misconceptions regarding the unhealthy and poisonous properties of tomatoes. As a result, many American colonists — especially those settled in the mid-Atlantic or New England regions without much Spanish influence — maintained the same erroneous conceptions about unhealthy or poisonous properties of the tomato through the 17th and into the 18th centuries. The flavor and versatility of the tomato, the impact of the Spanish cuisine, and the cultivation success in southern American colonies, all eventually began to break down and eradicate the British-based ideas about the tomato's toxicity. However, records show some persistence of these ideas even into the 19th century.

Modern folklore contains an often-repeated story about a New Jersey colonist, Robert Gibbon Johnson, who is reported to have made a stand for the tomato on the steps of the Salem, New Jersey Courthouse in 1820. Johnson, who was a notable leader of the Salem community, allegedly brought some tomato seeds from Britain, grew his tomatoes, then stood in front of a crowd on the courthouse steps and — to the great amazement of his town folk — ate his tomatoes. As the story goes, the gathered crowd was amazed that Johnson was not poisoned and did not die. This event was said to have kindled the American love for the tomato and helped to begin the growth of the tomato's popularity. This story has been repeated and rewritten countless times as fact, even by some credible news organizations. While it does make for a very good tomato tale, Andrew Smith put the matter to rest in his well-researched book, *The Tomato in America*, pointing out the many inconsistencies in, and the lack of, credible substantiation of the story.

 **Tomato Tidbits**

Chef Boyardee was actually a real chef. He was an Italian immigrant, Hector Boiardi, who popularized a tomato-based spaghetti sauce in his restaurant in Cleveland, before starting to sell the sauce under the Americanized version of his name.

Modern History of the American Tomato

Vegetable or fruit

Is the tomato a vegetable or a fruit? The answer is actually either one. From a botanical perspective, the tomato is a fruit. In a botanical sense, a fruit is a ripened ovary containing eggs or seeds that can go on to produce new plants. More specifically, the tomato is characterized botanically as a berry because it is a simple fruit produced from a single ovary. Generally speaking, a seed-containing structure that comes from a flower is designated as a fruit. In a this context, cucumbers, squash, pumpkins, peppers, corn, eggplants, beans, and peas are all designated as fruits.

Conversely, there is no botanical definition for a vegetable. "Vegetable" is a more colloquial than scientific term, used to describe an edible part of a plant that is not particularly sweet and is generally eaten as part of a meal versus as a snack or a dessert. In typical culinary practices, vegetables are more likely to be cooked than fruits, which are typically eaten raw. Obviously, these definitions have many exceptions and variations. As it is more a culinary than scientific term, the word "vegetable" is applied differently in different cultures and can be applied to items as diverse as tomatoes, mushrooms, onions, or ginger.

In legal terms, the tomato officially became a vegetable in 1893 when the United States Supreme Court ruled, in Nix v. Hedden, that the tomato was a vegetable. This was a significant issue in 1893 and became worthy of Supreme Court attention, when the Nix family, who were interested in importing tomatoes, cleverly tried to have tomatoes classified as fruits instead of vegetables, to avoid United States import tariffs. The Nixes were not successful in this effort, and the Supreme Court decided that tomatoes, peppers, squash, pumpkins, and a variety of other botanical fruits be legally classified as vegetables. This was a victory for both common language and the American farmers.

In the words of Supreme Court Justice Horace Gray, writing for the majority decision:

"Botanically speaking, tomatoes are the fruit of a vine, just as are cucumbers, squashes, beans, and peas. But in the common language of the people, whether sellers or consumers of provisions, all these are vegetables which are grown in kitchen gardens, and which, whether eaten cooked or raw, are, like potatoes, carrots, parsnips, turnips, beets, cauliflower, cabbage, celery, and lettuce, usually served at dinner in, with, or after the soup, fish, or meats which constitute the principal part of the repast, and not, like fruits generally, as dessert."

Campbell's® Tomato Soup

The popularity of the tomato was given a significant boost around the turn of the century by what was then known as the Campbell Preserve Company. The nephew of the company's general manager had recently graduated with a degree in chemistry from the

Massachusetts Institute of Technology, and had earned a Ph.D. from the University of Göttingen (in the city of Göttingen, Germany), and was looking for work. John T. Dorrance joined the company in 1897 and got to work on soup recipes. He invented a process for making condensed soup that saved shipping and storage costs and allowed Campbell to reduce the soup price from 30 cents to 10 cents. Campbell's Tomato Soup was introduced to the market in 1912 and quickly became a customer favorite. Based on the success of tomato soup and others, including chicken, vegetable, and oxtail, the name of the company was changed to Campbell Soup Company in 1922. During World War I, almost half of the company sales were attributed to the combination of Campbell's Tomato Soup and Campbell's Tomato Juice.

Campbell's influence on the tomato expanded when they decided in the early 1900s, to start growing their own produce in an effort to control and standardize quality. They began growing Jersey tomatoes from their own seeds to produce tomatoes for their soups. Campbell's has continued an active tomato breeding and development program. The company develops hundreds of varieties every year, allowing them to choose for key taste and processing attributes. Campbell's has even promoted their soups and commitment to agriculture by occasionally offering free Campbell tomato seeds when you purchase a can of soup.

As evidence of the iconic nature of both Campbell's soup (and in particular their tomato soup), American pop artist Andy Warhol immortalized the soup, the brand, and the can in 1962, with his famous Campbell soup can collection, the first of which is Tomato Soup. Warhol painted a series of 32 prints with realistic illustrations of 32 varieties of the Campbell's soups. This series of paintings was quite distinctive and is significant enough now, to be on permanent display at the New York City Museum of Modern Art. Just like the tomato itself, the classic red and white can is recognized in countries around the world and has, in appearance anyway, changed little in the last 100 years.

American breeding and development

In America and in Europe, growers began to select seeds of particular tomato subspecies that had desirable characteristics. During the 19th and 20th centuries, a large number of tomato varieties were chosen, nurtured, and propagated. Like most domesticated species, tomatoes are naturally self-pollinating and as a result, seeds from the plants will continue to produce plants that mimic the parents for generations. Early domestication and breeding was a matter of selecting seeds among the natural variations for individual plants that delivered a desired quality of a fruit or plant. Generally, the early focus for breeding was to achieve tomatoes that were large, red, round, and smooth. As the original tomato had a large amount of genetic diversity, there is now an enormous variety of colors, shapes, sizes, and tastes in the tomato portfolio, particularly among heirloom tomatoes.

One key milestone in the breeding and cultivation of tomatoes was the discovery of an individual seedling in a tomato field in Florida in 1914 that had the classic compact structure of a determinate plant. "Determinate" means the plant growth was self-stopping and tended to develop into more of a bush-style plant, versus the long, vine-style structure that continued to grow until killed by disease or frost. This plant was the result of a natural genetic mutation, but was quickly selected by growers for further propagation. All plants grown before this point had, like the wild varieties, been "indeterminate" with vine-type structures. This new determinate came to be called the Cooper Special, named after the company that initially marketed it. This discovery made possible the development of an array of future determinant varieties, which are now found in commercial and home gardens. Seeds of the Cooper Special variety are still available on the market today.

Another key milestone in tomato breeding history is the development of hybrid tomatoes. A hybrid combines the traits of different mother and father plants to produce a new plant, ideally with the best properties of each. In the world of vegetables, tomatoes are very easy to crossbreed and produce hybrids, so some gardeners and scientists were producing hybrid tomatoes in the 1800s. As hybrid development progressed in the 1900s, the superiority of the hybrids for particular desirable traits — including size, yield, shelf life, and taste — drove the broad use of hybrid varieties by essentially all tomato growers. Hybrids have also become very popular for home growers and dominate the catalogues of the major seed manufacturers. *More information about hybrid tomatoes is included in Chapter 2.*

Tomatoes may be the only vegetable to serve as the basis for a movie that became a cult comedy classic. *The Attack of the Killer Tomatoes* was made in 1978 and was popular enough to justify three sequels.

Genetic engineering began to play a role in tomato development in the later part of the 20th century. Especially notable is the fact that the tomato was the first complete food crop in which a genetically engineered product was brought to market. The tomato was called the "Flavr Savr" and was brought to market in 1994. The Flavr Savr was actually quite amazing, in that the modified gene added to the tomato, extended the shelf life of the tomato by three to four weeks. This additional shelf life allowed commercial growers to pick fruit much later in the ripening process, so the tomatoes survived better in the grocery store than tomatoes that were picked green. While the Flavr Savr was a technical success and initially generated much consumer interest, yield and cost disadvantages of the new tomato eventually led to its downfall. Another genetically engineered paste-type of tomato was introduced in the United Kingdom around the same time, but eventually met the same fate. In this case, an increasing European consumer reluctance to embrace genetic engineering partly drove the downfall. The commercial production of these tomatoes stopped at the turn of the 21st century.

Chapter 2:
Tomato Varieties Explained

The Anatomy of the Tomato Plant and Fruit

Tomatoes are commonly thought to be annuals, as they complete their growth and reproductive process in less than one year — seed to seed, so to speak. They are actually perennials in the right circumstances and climate. In their native climates in South America, wild tomato plants continue to grow from year to year. In most climates, they are typically short-lived perennials due to disease, frost, or a combination of the two, so they often grow as annuals.

Tomato plants are characterized as dicotyledons, referring to the two faux leaves (cotyledons) that emerge when the seed germinates. The cotyledons are simple, with smooth edges, and have a very different shape than what the true leaves of the plant have. Growth habit varies among the many different varieties of tomatoes from small compact bushes to long vines that, if unsupported, will eventually spread along the ground (decumbent). Unpruned tomato plants tend to have a main stem that dominates growth and inhibits the growth of lateral branches. However, once the primary stem flowers, growth in this main stem terminates and lateral branches begin to grow more aggressively.

Tomato plants are sometimes characterized by their leaf type. The most common type of leaf — which most people readily identify with tomato plants — are called regular leaves and have distinctive serrated edges. The leaf color can be many variations of green. They are lobed and can be compound, meaning they are a collection of smaller leaflets. The other type of tomato plant leaf is called a potato leaf, as it resembles the leaves of the potato plant. These leaves have smooth edges and usually have no lobes. They are typically darker green. In both types, hairs and glands called trichomes appear on the surface of the leaves and stem of the tomato plant. These hairs are responsible for the rapid and easy rooting that is typical of tomato plants. The trichome glands are the organs responsible for the characteristic and strong odor typically associated with tomato plants.

The root of the tomato plant is typically of the 'taproot' variety. The taproot is a primary larger root that is parallel to the main stem and runs fairly deep. Lateral roots will branch off the taproot and sublateral roots will also branch off the lateral roots. The taproot anatomy is important to the structural integrity of the tomato. It is also important in reaching depths of soil to maintain moisture for the plant in times of minimal water. If new plants are rooted from a branch or stem — rather than grown from seed — the root system will be of the fibrous type, meaning that a main taproot does not exist and the roots are thin and branching, forming a mat-type structure. Roots also have surface hairs that are important in the transport of water and nutrients up and down the plant.

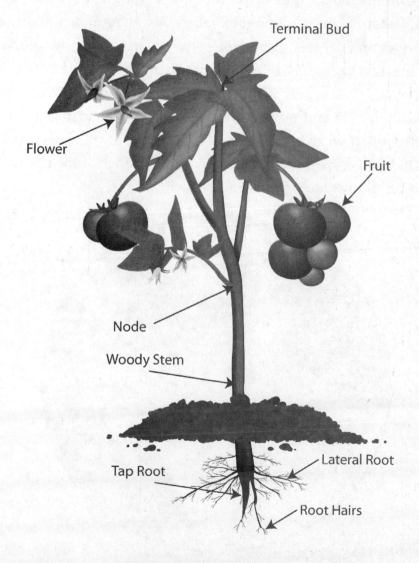

DIAGRAM 1: TOMATO PLANT

Tomato plants in full bloom have yellow flowers and can occur in singular or with multiple flowers in a group. As in all flowers, the brightly colored petals serve to attract pollinators, such as bumblebees. Within the colored petals of the flower, there are multiple stamen, which are the male organs of the flower and the source of pollen granules. The stamen are generally fused together and surround the female part of the tomato flowers. The female part of the tomato plant is sometimes called the ovary and consists of the ovules and carpels. The ovule is the organ that, with pollination and fertilization, will eventually develop into the seeds of the tomato. The carpels are green, bulb-type structures that surround the ovule and eventually develop into the locules of the tomato fruit. If you dissect a tomato flower, the number of carpels you find will correspond to the eventual number of locules that will be in the tomato fruit.

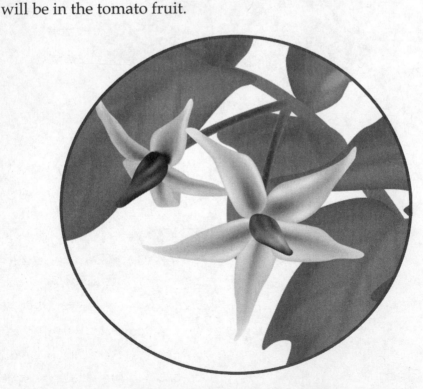

DIAGRAM 2: TOMATO FLOWER

Fertilization occurs when the pollen granules, produced by the stamen, travel down inside the female organ of the flower and meet up with the ovule. Most varieties of modern tomatoes — and almost all commercial varieties — are self-pollinating. Self-pollination means the pollen of a flower on a particular plant pollinates that same flower or other flowers on the same plant. In these cases, pollination does not require the services of bumblebees, but does require some motion; either from the natural movement of the wind or, in the case of greenhouse plants, assistance from a vibration mechanism. Other less-common varieties of tomato plants require pollen from another flower variety; these require the assistance of flying insects. If the tomato flower is not fertilized, the flower will wilt, die, and separate from the plant. If the flower is fertilized, the ovule begins cell division and slow growth, which lasts for two to three weeks. Afterward, the growth rate accelerates until about the five-week point, when the fruit reaches its full size. At this point, the green pigment in the tomato begins to fade, and orange and red pigments begin to develop.

The fruit of the tomato plant consists of a fleshy or meaty supporting structure called the pericarp, which encases the locules. There may be two or multiple locules and as previously mentioned, these correspond to the number of carpels that were found in the tomato flower. Most cultivated tomatoes have four or five locules, but some have as many as ten. The locules contain the seeds of the tomato, and the number of seeds varies with the tomato variety. This can also vary, to some extent, within individuals of a particular plant or variety. All fertilized ovules do not necessarily make the full transition to tomato seed. In young tomatoes, the material within the locules that surrounds the seeds is relatively dense, but as the fruit matures, this material becomes more gelatinous and watery.

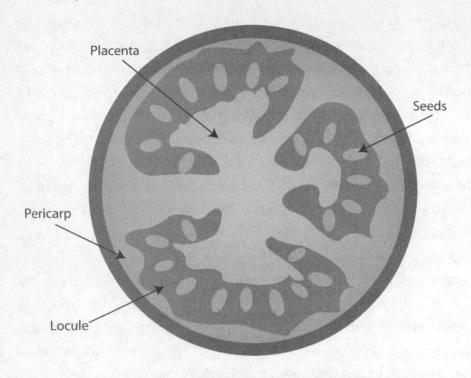

Placenta

Seeds

Pericarp

Locule

DIAGRAM 3: TOMATO FRUIT SECTION
OF A THREE LOCULE FRUIT

CASE STUDY: WHAT'S THE DIFF? SAM COX TALKS HYBRID AND HEIRLOOM

Sam Cox
Colorado State University Department of Horticulture
Currently with USDA Agricultural Research Service

Creating a hybrid tomato is pretty easy because tomatoes are naturally homozygous and do not outcross. Translating these genetic terms to backyard, gardener language, this means the children of tomato plants tend to have the characteristics of their parents, and parents tend to mate with themselves. To create a hybrid, one has to open up the flower before the pollen matures, remove the male organ (anthers), and apply pollen from another tomato line. It is difficult to say when the first tomato hybrid was created, but it was certainly well over 100 years ago. Folks do it now, even in their own backyards.

Heirloom tomatoes, on the other hand, do not need the extra attention. They pollinate themselves without all the fuss. The reason they are called heirlooms is because they do pollinate themselves and breed true from generation to generation, without any outside help. This creates flavor, texture, and color traits that are consistent across generations — an "heirloom." Some seed companies do not particularly like heirloom varieties; therefore, they aggressively market hybrid cultivars. Once a customer buys heirloom seeds, they will never need to buy a seed of that variety again because all the seed produced from that original seed will be genetically identical. While it is possible for a tomato to be pollinated by another tomato plant that might be of a different variety, it is extremely unlikely that pollen from another flower will beat pollen coming from within the same flower. I would guess that greater than 99 percent of heirloom flowers are self-pollinated.

Heirloom versus Hybrid

It is probably useful here to describe the botanical difference between heirloom tomatoes and hybrid tomatoes, as it is largely a matter of pollination mechanisms. Hybrid tomatoes are carefully bred to select for a specific group of tomato characteristics. Colloquially speaking, growers will thoughtfully choose a mother plant and a father plant with the desired characteristics, to produce fruit with seeds that ideally combine the best of both of these parents. Simplistically, this might be a mother plant that produces a very big fruit and a father plant that produces a very sweet fruit. Pollen grains from the father plant are used to pollinate and hopefully fertilize flowers on the mother plant. The resulting tomatoes produced by this mother plant are then harvested to collect the seeds for the new big and sweet cultivar. The word 'cultivar' is used in referring to hybrids, which are deliberately crossed to produce specific offspring. In cases of accidental cross-pollination or mutation that produces a new offspring, it is referred to as a new variety. In principle and in practice, this has been a wonderful system for breeding and continuing to breed excellent qualities into the current portfolio of tomato cultivars. Most people would agree that the tomatoes of today are better in culinary quality than original wild tomatoes, due in part to the influence of hybridization. *Heirloom tomatoes will be described in full detail in Chapter 10.*

Hybrid seed production sounds very simple, but in commercial practice is tedious and labor intensive. Most modern tomato plants have a general tendency to self-pollinate easily; the growers must emasculate (remove the male pollinating organs) of the flowers of the mother plant to prevent self-pollination. There is also an intricate and painstaking process for collecting pollen from the father plants and, at just the right time, adding this pollen to the mother flowers. Nonetheless, the improvement of some key desired tomato properties has made this effort worthwhile.

The rub for the home gardener is that in the world of hybridization, the seeds generated by this hybridization do not consistently provide future generations. The seeds of this new, big, and sweet fruit cannot always be saved and germinated for the next season. The grower will typically get tomato fruit, but the degree to which it is identical to the original fruit varies. As successive generations of the hybrid seed are gathered and replanted, the fruit produced tends to quickly drift back to the characteristics of one of the parent plants. The only option you have to get identical big and sweet fruit is to go back to the seed vendors and buy new hybrid seeds.

However, heirloom tomatoes are open and often self-pollinated. When an heirloom tomato plant is self-pollinated, the seeds for the next season do, in fact, provide for successful growth of future generations of the heirloom. This has allowed serious and traditional gardeners to save and preserve some unique and interesting varieties over the years. One of the challenges with self-pollination, however, is that cross-pollination can occur. This means the pollen of another male tomato plant variety located within the general area can make its way to the specific heirloom female plant and create a potentially new variety that is not necessarily the desired variety.

Specific botanical definitions aside, heirloom tomatoes are generally defined as tomato varieties that are not hybrids and have been passed down through generations. In the United Kingdom, where they are called Heritage tomatoes, an equivalent interest in this type of tomato has emerged over the last decade or so. Hybrid tomatoes are generally grown and bred by corporations or large seed or agricultural enterprises. While a large number of hybrid varieties exist, they still tend to fall into a relatively small window of broadly popular styles and types. On the other hand, heirlooms are found in an enormous range of colors, sizes, and shapes, some of which you might not immediately recognize as tomatoes. *For more information on the advantages, disadvantages, and unique challenges of hybrids and heirlooms, see Chapter 10.*

Indeterminate versus Determinate Varieties

Tomatoes are characterized as either determinate or indeterminate. In both cases, the creation of a flower terminates the growth of a particular shoot. In the case of the indeterminate type, when a flower terminates the shoot's growth, the plant has the capacity to develop branches that will continue the growth of the plant. This branching can continue indefinitely; therefore, indeterminate varieties tend to grow into taller, leggier-type plants. As a result, they require more attention in supporting and managing. Some of these varieties have been bred and cultivated to grow into what are essentially tomato trees, towering 20 to 30 feet tall. These plants are coaxed to grow literally hundreds of pounds of tomatoes per plant.

Determinates have very limited branching capability and tend to develop into the form of a more compact bush. They also flower earlier and set all their flowers within a shorter period of time. Most determinate varieties will produce ripe tomatoes in 60 to 70 days from transplant, while the indeterminate varieties have a transplant to ripe fruit time of 70 to 85 days. Most seed catalogs and Web sites will include in the seed description the expected number of days from transplant in the garden to ripe fruit. Determinate type plants are preferred for commercial growing, where machine-picking and handling is important. The determinate type is also preferred when the major objective is canning or freezing because all the fruit can be managed in a short period of time. In contrast, the indeterminate varieties will continue to grow, flower, and produce fruit until the plant is killed by disease or frost. For this reason, indeterminate varieties are preferred when the objective is a long growing season with a continuous supply of tomatoes.

This classification of tomatoes into determinate and indeterminate is not totally clean. There are also a number of varieties that are sometimes classified as semi-determinates. These plants tend to form taller, but still bush-shaped plants and will produce a second crop of tomatoes after the first.

Four General Tomato Types

If you choose to start tomato plants from seed, there are hundreds of tomato varieties from which to choose. There are a number of ways to organize and make sense of the varieties — climate preference, disease resistance, and size are some examples. But given that the purpose of growing tomatoes is to eat them, the following approach focuses on the culinary end uses that you most likely have in mind for your tomatoes.

Slicers

These tomatoes are picked fresh from the garden, sliced, and eaten soon after picking. These will be the source of those fresh tomato sandwiches, side dishes of sliced tomatoes, or the foundation of insalata caprese; a fresh mozzarella, basil, and tomato combination that is drizzled with balsamic vinegar. As this group of tomatoes will be eaten all season long, they tend to be indeterminate. Also, this group of tomatoes is prized most for flavor, so the group often has the highest sugar content. Some of the varieties you might find in this category include:

Better Boy: This is a classic tomato variety that has been a standard favorite variety for decades. It is indeterminate, disease-resistant, produces large smooth fruit, and is firm and meaty, so it slices easily. This variety is notable not only for its longevity, but also for being the tomato variety that produced a Guinness World Records plant — with a production of 342 pounds per plant.

Beefmaster: This variety produces some of the largest tomatoes, with fruit that weigh up to 2 pounds. It is an indeterminate variety that is resistant to cracking. It is not a perfectly round fruit, but has light ribbing, particularly around the top. The ribbed shape and its large size make it unsuitable for machine processing. This type can handle a variety of climates as long as the growing season is not too short.

Super Beefsteak: This is a variety that resembles the Beefmaster. It is rounder but not as large, averaging about 1 pound. It is an indeterminate variety that produces large meaty fruit with a good flavor and slices well.

Bush Early Girl: This is a determinate variety designed for delivering early tomato plants. These plants are targeted to produce plants up to two weeks earlier than the typical indeterminate tomato plant. This particular variety produces fairly large fruit on very compact bushes that would be appropriate for container plantings as well as in the garden.

Long Keeper: This is an interesting variety that is semi-determinate. These tomatoes are very slow to ripen. Growers design them to be picked just before harvest, when they are a mild pink color, to store over the winter. Some gardeners report storing these tomatoes for up to five months after harvest in cool, dark conditions. While the flavor may not approach summer vine-ripe varieties, it is still much superior to grocery store winter tomatoes.

Stuffers

This group of tomatoes is selected for a specific anatomy: a seed cluster that is easily removed. This cluster makes this tomato perfect for recipes that call for hot- or cold-stuffing. This group of tomatoes is similar to original wild tomatoes because they are not fleshy throughout the fruit. While they typically have a nice flavor, this group is bred more for their firm flesh, which can hold up well to stuffing and baking.

Red Stuffer: This is an indeterminate variety targeted for stuffing. The fruit is red or orange in color and has three to four sections that can easily be removed. This tomato has a center seed cluster similar to the structure of a bell pepper. It has a mild taste that will not overwhelm the flavor of the stuffing and the overall dish it is complimenting.

Yellow Stuffer Tomato: This is an indeterminate prolific variety that has the classic stuffer center-seed cluster and has the four distinct lobes of a bell pepper. The fruit is a bright yellow, which complements a variety of stuffing options.

Striped Cavern: This is an indeterminate variety with a focus on shape and structure rather than flavor. It produces a small- to medium-sized red fruit with yellow stripes. The thick wall and interesting lobed shape make it perfect for stuffing.

Sauce tomatoes

This is a group of tomatoes that are well suited for making sauces and pastes or for canning and preserving. These tomatoes have a fleshy, meaty texture with low water content. They are often determinate varieties. When preserving or making sauces, the ripening of many tomatoes at once — as is typical with determinates — is a real benefit because the cooking and preserving process is much more efficient when done in bulk. While scientists developed the following varieties for use in sauces, almost any tomato in the garden can make a delightful tomato sauce. When tomatoes are prolific in the garden and you do not want them to go to waste, practicality overcomes purity of intent.

San Marzano: This indeterminate variety is a type of plum tomato and has a somewhat longer season than typical sauce tomatoes. They were popularized near San Marzano, Italy, and are a popular commercial variety. They have a somewhat pointy shape and a strong, somewhat bittersweet taste.

Roma: This is a determinate variety and is the type of plum tomato often found in the grocery store. The plant is a compact bush that produces a lot of fruit, so it is popular in commercial gardening or with home gardeners who do a lot of canning or preserving.

Shady Lady: This is a determinate variety that grows into a fairly large vine with quite a lot of foliage, hence the name. The red fruit is medium to large and round. This variety is very popular in California, the home of most commercial sauce growth and production in the United States, for both commercial farms and farmers' markets.

Heinz 1439: This is a determinate variety that — as is indicated from its name — was developed by the H. J. Heinz Company researchers as part of their effort to produce better tomatoes for canning sauces and pastes. It produces a round, red medium-sized tomato with relatively large seeds.

Big Mama: This is an indeterminate variety with the classic oblong shape of other sauce tomatoes, but is notable for its large size. Individual fruits can be up to 5 inches long and 3 inches across.

Small salad tomatoes

This is the category of tomatoes dominated by grape and cherry varieties; popular for salads, vegetable trays, and snacking. The grape tomato strain was first created in Southeast Asia and was introduced to the American market in the late 1990s. The grape tomato is smaller and tends to be more oblong than round, like the cherry tomato. It also has lower water content and a thicker skin than the cherry tomato, so there is less of a "squirt" risk. Cherry and grape tomatoes have distinctly different tastes and appeal to different palates. All varieties in this category are extremely prolific, generally producing far more salad tomatoes per plant than you will have salads to consume them with. Small tomato varieties also seem to be the most disease- and frost-resistant, generally lasting longer into the fall than other larger tomato varieties.

Gardener's Delight Cherry: This is a prolific cherry tomato plant that produces high yields right up until the first frost. It is an indeterminate plant that continues to grow and can easily produce vines up to 10 feet long if not pruned. The fruit of this variety tends to be crack resistant. Cracking or splitting of the fruit tends to be more common with high-water-content varieties like the cherry tomatoes.

Sweet Baby Girl Cherry: This is a determinate cherry tomato plant, but grows on somewhat smaller bushes than typical cherry tomatoes. The plant produces dark red cherry tomatoes that are smaller and somewhat sweeter than the average. The fruit is round and bright red.

Tiny Tim: This is a determinate cherry variety that only grows up to about 18 inches tall and can be grown in pots as small as 6 inches, making it perfect for sunny spots in a window or on a porch.

Napa Grape: This is an indeterminate variety prized for its sweetness. The fruit are small and ripen earlier than most small varieties. These are produced on relatively large-vined plants.

Sprite #5025 Grape: This is a determinate variety; therefore, it tends to form a smaller, compact bush appropriate for container planting on a deck or porch. This plant produces small, red, oval grape tomatoes in large quantity.

Other specialty tomatoes

With tomato breeding being a relatively easy exercise even for the novice gardener, there are an enormous number of tomato varieties for specific purposes — some useful, some just interesting.

Granny Smith: This is an interesting indeterminate variety of tomato that is green to light yellow when ripe. It is very firm, which makes it a good selection for grilling or frying. It also keeps well after harvest. It is a fun alternative to picking green, unripe versions of other tomatoes to use in green tomato recipes.

Arkansas Traveler #3566: This is an indeterminate variety prized for its heat resistance and ability to produce fruit late into the season. The University of Arkansas bred this type, and it produces medium-sized pink fruit.

Early Girl VFF Hybrid #2783: The classic tomato plant that produces early in the season has an amazing 52 days from transplant to harvest. It does well in a variety of climates and produces small red fruit.

Health Kick: Another interesting variety that was bred to have a high level of lycopene, a natural antioxidant. The fruit has 50 percent more lycopene than the average tomato. This determinate plant produces an abundance of medium-sized fruit.

Tomato Tumbler: This is a determinate variety of cherry tomatoes that is unique, as it is bred to adapt well to hanging baskets. It produces a small, sweet, bright red fruit.

Oregon Spring: This is a cold-resistant variety developed by Oregon State University for short season gardeners. It is a determinate variety that grows on a small compact bush. It is good for slicing and also good for producing a thick creamy juice.

Delicious Tomato: This is an indeterminate variety, and its known as being the variety that produced the tomato that won a Guinness World Records record for the heaviest tomato. This particular individual tomato weighed a hefty 7 pounds. The Delicious Tomato is meaty, with minimal seeds and grows large, crack-resistant fruit.

Selecting Tomatoes for the Garden

Given this description of the botanical life of the tomato plant and the array of varieties possible to grow in a garden, how do you choose which varieties are right for your garden? Obviously this is a broad question with myriad answers, which depend on many factors, including space constraints, interests in tomato preserving, culinary tastes, local climate, and the amount of time you are willing or able to commit to the effort. While it is impossible to answer this question with a broad response for all people, it is possible to offer a few principles to guide in your initial choices. As your experience and confidence in tomato gardening grows, your choices will become more refined and more tailored to your personal gardening profile. The following are suggestions and things to consider, in order to help you determine which tomato varieties you would prefer to plant in your garden.

Choose the right number of plants. If the objective is to grow fresh tomatoes for eating throughout the summer, a reasonable estimate for planting would be two to three of the slicer variety of plants per household member, and one cherry or grape tomato plant for the family. However, if you are also interested in preserving tomatoes for the winter, you can add two sauce-type tomato plants for every member of the household. With this kind of planning, in any given year, conditions might produce an overabundance of tomatoes or just enough to get by.

Mix and match. Choose a few reliable hybrids that can be counted on for flavor, yield, and disease resistance. Include at least one small salad variety. Also, add a few heirloom types or more exotic varieties for some visual and taste diversity to the menu.

Target for fresh tomatoes all season long. Add a few plants to the collection that are early and late-season varieties to extend the season. The particular varieties you choose will depend on your local climate, but there are various early and late season varieties and season-extending techniques, to extend your tomato season to its longest timeframe.

Experiment through the seasons. Tomatoes can be finicky tenants in your garden, as they are subject to local climate and soil conditions, which are out of your control as a gardener. Be willing to give up on varieties that do not seem able to deliver, and remain open to trying new options that might be more successful in your local conditions.

Chapter 3:
Selecting a Site and Improving the Soil

Where to Grow Tomatoes

Tomatoes are one of the easiest foods to grow because of several factors, such as:

- Tomato seeds have a very high and reliable germination rate.

- Many varieties are bred with resistance to typical plant diseases.

- They are reasonably adaptable to a variety of climates.

- They mature and produce fruit fairly rapidly.

Nonetheless, the control and management of variables, such as site selection and soil condition, can make the difference between a marginal crop and a bountiful one. This chapter focuses on

key considerations in choosing the best site for tomato plants and in making the soil in the site optimum. A key theme that runs throughout this discussion is planning ahead. The time to think about site selection and optimization is not the week before you plant. There are a number of preparatory factors you can take care of during the previous fall and winter, which will contribute to a better crop and potentially save you time and money.

CASE STUDY: GARDENING ENTHUSIAST ON GROWING IN DIFFERENT CLIMATES

Fritz Radwanski
Lifetime Gardener
Hudson, Ohio

Fritz Radwanski has been gardening since he was a child. He has lived and worked in a number of different areas of the country. While he left old sofas behind from time to time in his moves, his tomato garden always followed along. He is a big fan of space-intensive gardening.

"I have yet to live anywhere where you couldn't grow a tomato," Radwanski said. "I have had gardens in Wisconsin, Georgia, and Ohio. Each area has its pros and cons." While the temperatures always come to mind first as a major difference in growing vegetables between northern and southern states, Radwanski said the northern latitudes do contribute ample sunlight in the growing season. He said he gets about an hour of extra sunlight per day during the growing season in Wisconsin than he did while living in Georgia. "That compensates a little for the late start," Radwanski said. "Of course, there are always trade-offs wherever you are."

For example, when it finally gets warm in northern Ohio and Wisconsin, there is a burst of activity to get all the plants in, he said. In the south, everything is planted earlier and they spread crop planting out over months. However, in the north, once the garden is in, you can relax a bit. In the south, you are constantly on the watch for worms, aphids, and disease. Also, you seem to spend more time watering and taking care of the soil. On the other hand, in the south, it is a blessing to have a longer season to enjoy the garden, Radwanski said.

With respect to tomato varieties, Radwanski has tried many options in the various climates he has gardened in. "I have tried all kinds of exotic varieties, but I keep coming back to the standards — Better Boys, Early Girls, Rutgers, Roma tomatoes," he said. "I tend to avoid the ones with super-large fruits, as they aren't as productive as other smaller fruited varieties if you are trying to grow in a high-intensity, limited space approach. The larger fruited varieties also grow on very prolific, long vines that are more difficult to train and manage."

Radwanski does have a fondness for the taste of Northern tomatoes. "I'm not sure what the reason is, but I just think the Northern tomatoes taste sweeter," he said. "Maybe the extra cloud cover or the cooler days in July and August contribute something. Or maybe the more steady moisture that the tomato experiences in Wisconsin or Ohio versus the South is the reason, but I am convinced they just taste sweeter in the North."

Light requirements

While tomatoes are warm-weather crops and flourish in warm, sunny sites, choosing a site to optimize for light requirements is not always as obvious as it may sound. Studies have shown fruit production can be four to five times higher with optimal lighting conditions. Greenhouse growers, who can more accurately control the level of lighting and more effectively reach lower plant leaves as well as upper leaves, have better production yields than field growers, largely as a result of this ability to control light.

Tomatoes will certainly not flourish under low or inadequate light conditions. Fewer tomatoes will be produced, and the crop will ripen later than predicted for that variety. In other words, tomato plants grown in low light conditions will produce, but it will not be the best or the biggest harvest possible. The primary signal that your plants may not be getting sufficient light is the height and legginess of the plants. Under low-light conditions, plants will quickly grow long and thinner vines with less amount of foliage and few flowers. In addition, sometimes the color of the plant will fade to a lighter or inconsistent green.

Conversely, high-light intensity — particularly after fruit has appeared — can be as damaging to tomato plants as low light is. Hot, late summer days with low humidity and no cloud cover can contribute to scalded or cracked fruit. Although not always easy to manage, some partial shade in the middle of the day will help relieve potential damage that excess light can create. Producing healthy plants with lots of foliage early in the season, to help shade developing fruit, can lessen the impact of too much light later in the season.

It is common to find recommendations of choosing a site with a minimum of six to eight hours of sunlight per day. Tomatoes are grown across the United States, in geographies with a broad range of cloud cover, fog, average temperatures, and humidity. Therefore, specifying a number of full sun hours per day can be an efficient general rule of tomato gardeners. However, this is also somewhat of an over-simplification. You can most successfully define the best site in your area over a period of time, by making an educated first estimate of site selection and then letting your experience guide you the next year. In selecting your site, recognize that the light a particular area sees changes dramatically during the season and can change over the years.

As trees around the area grow more foliage and grow taller and broader, what might have been an adequate site five years ago may no longer be so. While cutting down offending trees may not always be a viable option, cutting particular branches may have a big impact on your garden without meaningfully impacting the tree. Proximity to trees can also be problematic; not only due to the impact of shading, but also due to encroaching tree root structures, which can make tilling difficult and will also compete aggressively for soil moisture in dry periods. Removing roots is an option, but this can be labor intensive and can also compromise tree stability and integrity. Always consider the movement of the sun across the sky as the season develops. By the end of the season, the sun will have moved to a southern path in the sky. Structures that did not impact your garden at all in May can start to have a major impact in August.

Wind protection

Cold spring winds can be a challenge to the vigor of newly transplanted tomato seedlings, especially in more northern climates. Later in the season, as the plants grow tall and become heavy with fruit, wind — or the combination of wind and heavy rain — can contribute to unstable plants that are easily toppled, even after supporting. Winds can also aggravate moisture loss in the garden, particularly if mulch is not used. If possible, it is best to look for a site where there is some protection from these winds. The protection can be natural, such as a woodsy or tree-covered section in the area upwind of the tomato garden, or a hillside similarly situated. The protection might also be in the form of man-made structures. Choosing your site so the tomato garden is downwind from wooden fencing or downwind from other home or garage structures can have a big impact on how much your seedlings are affected by cold spring winds.

One complicating factor is that wind protection often coincides with shade production. In this case, light requirements will always trump the desire to shield plants from the wind. One can manage around windy areas, but inadequate light is detrimental to successful gardening.

The total absence of wind is not necessarily a benefit, however. Light breezes are an important part of the pollinating process for tomato plants; particularly for heirloom varieties. It is known that in backyard greenhouses with adequate light and insufficient air movement, tomato blossoms can drop and tomato yields will plummet. This is well recognized in the tomato business, and commercial greenhouse growers have numerous strategies for either creating their own wind or simulating it with other mechanisms to assure adequate pollination. In the same way that growing tomatoes indoors can limit pollination, an overly protected outdoor site can also reduce or restrict pollination.

Erosion control

As you would expect, level ground generally offers the best defense against soil erosion. However, level ground may not offer the best combination of light or soil conditions that other, more-sloping areas can. In cases where growing on a slope makes sense based on other considerations, terracing can be a successful approach to consider. A combination of terraces and raised beds can be both a practical and an aesthetically appealing approach to a hilly terrain. In many cases, a hilly terrain is a feature of cooler climates, and terracing offers warming advantages for cooler climates. Cool air will tend to move down the slope rather than settling on the terrace garden. To increase sunlight hours, the best place for a sloping garden is on a south or southwest-facing slope. Terraces can be built with stone or wood and take a variety of forms, depending on the steepness of the slope. To limit erosion, add organic matter to reduce the density and improve the drainage of soil — this is very important in a hillside garden.

Contrary to this, low-lying areas may be level and free from erosion, but may not drain well. Tomatoes do not do well with wet feet, so steer away from areas that tend to regularly collect standing water in rainy times. Standing water indicates low areas where the collected water has nowhere to go and it can also indicate non-porous, poor-draining soil that will not be conducive to growing tomatoes without substantial soil amendments. While adequate moisture is critical to healthy tomato plants and fruit, too much water can be just as damaging. Water in soil will replace air and, if persistently wet, the soil will have insufficient oxygen to support healthy root growth. Wet areas also tend to be locations with a propensity to harbor bacterial or fungal diseases, which can threaten tomatoes.

Other factors

The proximity of the garden to the kitchen is an often overlooked, but an important consideration. This is true not just for the obvious convenience of shorter trips from the picking to the cooking, but rabbits, deer, and other wildlife pests might think twice before snacking on garden produce that is closer to signs and sounds of human and pet life than a garden isolated from the main living area. This, of course, is not a guarantee of protection from wildlife, as deer and rabbits in more populated areas can become quite acclimated to people and pets. Nonetheless, it does add another level of deterrent that can be prove valuable.

Another consideration for site selection is rotation. Tomatoes, like many other crops planted in the same site each year, will eventually show signs of disease and blight, and productivity will diminish. Even more specifically, tomatoes should not be planted in locations where other plants of the same family were planted. Tomatoes are in the same family as peppers, eggplant, and potatoes, so if possible, avoid repeat planting of vegetables within this family. Planting tomatoes in the same location year after year can allow nematodes, insects, and disease-causing bacteria or fungus to persist. These troublemakers can survive up to three years in garden soil, and while the tomato plants may seem to get off to a good start in the spring, they will more easily and more often succumb to an early wilt or blight caused by these organisms. In addition, planting tomatoes in the same area can also deplete the soil of particular minerals or fertilizers that are important to tomato growth.

While rotation of crops is desirable and should be attempted by all, many home gardeners face a space limitation that will challenge their ability to do a meaningful rotation. If this is the case, it is all the more important to prevent the spread of disease in other ways. Remove any diseased plants from the garden and do not add them to the compost pile. Also, at the end of the season, remove old plants as soon as possible. Soil testing is even more important to ensure that the soil is not being depleted of necessary nutrients, and allow time to for the soil to be refortified. Finally, if crop rotation is out of the question, the selection of disease-resistant tomato varieties is even more important.

Soil Testing

The what and why of soil testing

It is a rare gardener who finds his new garden plot full of perfectly balanced soil, ideal for growing tomatoes and any other vegetables. Many areas of the country where tomatoes are grown start with sandy, clay, or rocky soils that need substantial improvement. Also, in many areas — especially suburban developed areas — much of the topsoil is removed in the construction process, leaving poor gardening material behind.

Despite the fact that testing soil is easy and relatively cheap, the vast majority of home gardeners rarely do it. This is especially true with new gardeners who tend to think of soil as generic dirt. Seasoned gardeners will appreciate the texture, feel, color, and smell of a well-composted, fertile, and loamy soil. Reluctance to test also has a lot to do with the general ease of tomato growing and the fact that tomato plants will produce at some level in a variety of different soils. Typical gardeners rarely appreciate how much more prolific their garden crops could be if they took the extra steps of getting an analytical assessment of their soil. Therefore, they could miss using this information to adjust soil amendments and fertilizers to optimize nutrients for tomatoes and other related garden vegetables. The specific kinds of tests used vary from region to region, but typical soil testing consists of the following general analyses:

Soil acidity or pH: As do many garden vegetables, tomatoes grow best in a soil that has a pH of between 6.2 and 6.8. The pH is the chemical measurement of the acidity or alkalinity of water or a water-based solution. In this case, pH will measure acidity in soil. The pH is measured on a scale of 0 to 14, with a pH of 7 defined as neutral. A measure of 7 means there are equal amounts of the two components of water: positive hydrogen ions (H+) and negative hydroxyl ions (OH-). An acidic medium has a preponderance of positive hydrogen ions, and an alkaline medium has a preponderance of negative hydroxyl ions. Tomatoes prefer a slightly acidic soil. Growers can test the pH at home with standard pH strips purchased from locations that sell pool supplies. While a lab testing result will be more accurate and precise, this home measurement is simple and inexpensive enough to be done frequently, and should be sensitive enough to at least give some guidance that the garden is moving in the right direction.

Phosphorous: Phosphorous is important to promote root growth in tomato plants. For this reason, it is particularly important for young seedlings and early transplants. This should ensure a strong root system that will support further plant growth.

Potassium: Potassium is important for healthy, heavy-fruiting tomato plants. For this reason, an appropriate level of potassium is important throughout the growing season. Potassium is very mobile in the soil and in the plants themselves, so levels of potassium can vary widely as a result of periods of heavy rains. Tomatoes need at least as much potassium as nitrogen in the soil for good development.

Other analyses: Depending on the particular extension service or laboratory that you choose, other secondary elements — including calcium, magnesium, and sulfur — may also be part of the testing protocol. Most of these elements come from decomposing organic matter.

Organic matter: This test is not usually standard, but many extension services offer it. There is debate about the value of this test; similar to the nitrogen test described later, the soil organic matter test is difficult to interpret. While organic matter is unequivocally a valued component of any soil, ideal targets for this measurement are difficult to define and can vary depending on other characteristics of the soil.

Nitrogen: Nitrogen is essential to almost every biochemical pathway in plant growth. Small changes in available nitrogen can result in large effects on yield, foliage growth, and the quality of fruit. Nitrogen is added to the soil directly via chemical fertilizers or added indirectly via a variety of organic materials. When added via organic materials, nitrogen in the organic material will be converted to nitrogen over time, which is available for uptake by the plant. When added to the soil through chemical fertilizers, the nitrogen is either added or quickly converted in the soil to the nitrate form (NO_3^-). The nitrate form is very soluble and is taken up by plants easily and washed through the soil quickly by heavy rains. Therefore, nitrogen levels can vary widely. For these reasons, nitrogen testing can be done, but is very difficult to interpret and is not often recommended for routine soil testing. As an alternative, gardeners tend to add a standard amount of organic matter or fertilizer to plants at prescribed times and judge results by the texture and feel of their soil and the performance of their plants.

When and how to test soil

The best time to collect samples for garden testing is in the off-season. This can be in the late fall after the garden has finished producing and is cleared, or it can be in the early spring after the first garden tilling. In a new garden, testing in the fall to identify appropriate amendments, amending the soil based on test results, and then testing again in early spring, is a good approach. Plan for collecting samples immediately after tilling because it offers the best chance for getting a representative sample of the soil through the top 1 to 8 inches of soil. It is important to collect a representative sample across the garden surface as well, so collect small, hand spade-sized samples from roughly eight locations across the garden. Mix all the samples together in a clean bucket and let the samples dry for several days. After drying, collect a few cups of the soil sample in a zipped plastic bag to send to the testing lab. Once the garden and your fertilizing, mulching, and soil amendments habits are established, soil-testing results will also stabilize. You can reduce testing frequency to once every three to five years.

Where testing is done

The first approach for testing is to consider going through your local state or county extension services. The Cooperative Extension Service is a nationwide nonprofit educational network that provides — among other things — gardening and agricultural information and advice for commercial and home growers on a local basis. Every state in the United States has at least a state office associated with a public state university, and many states have multiple county and local offices, in addition to the state office. In some states, extension services offer a wide array of testing services. In others, the extension services will have arrangements with or references to appropriate laboratories that specialize in soil testing. In most cases, test results will be reported as specific analytical measurements and, like typical analytical testing, will also denote target ideal ranges for your garden soil, so you can understand whether your measurements are low, high, or on target. *A list of public state universities that house this office as well as their corresponding Web sites is included in Appendix C.*

A less-desirable alternative for soil testing is to use kits sold in garden stores. These kits are reasonably inexpensive, can be used repeatedly, and give a general idea of soil pH and fertility. If you only test once or twice a year, testing with a local extension service is probably no more expensive than the garden kits. Local extension services also offer the advantage of having the tests done by experts who will not only give you more accurate results, but will also be able to interpret the results in light of typical local growing conditions and the specific crops that you want to grow.

Plant testing

Plant testing is another service offered through many state and county extension services or university agricultural services. This can be done for two purposes. The first is to identify visual symptoms of a suspected nutrient deficiency. Another is to identify nitrogen and other key nutrient components in the plant, as an indication of soil health. For plant analysis to be successful, plant samples should be collected as soon as symptoms start to appear. Sending the extension service a dead tissue will not provide for a useful diagnosis. Some extension services also appreciate photographs of plants in the garden to aid in the diagnostic process. Plant testing is not a replacement for soil testing, but can be done after soil modification and during the growing season as another indicator of adequate soil health. Even if an agricultural extension service is not located in your area, most agencies will provide sampling mailing kits as well as instructions for collecting and mailing samples for testing.

CASE STUDY: GROWING IN DIFFERENT CLIMATES

Jeff Schalau
Agent, Agriculture and
Natural Resources
The University of Arizona Cooperative
Extension Service

Jeff Schalau is an agent in the Cooperative Extension Service at the University of Arizona and has some experience in growing tomatoes in the hot, dry spring and summer of Arizona. Here, he talks about growing tomatoes in the diversity of climates found in his state.

Different growing climates have different opportunities and different challenges in growing tomatoes. One of the extremes in climate is probably the dry, hot climate of Arizona.

According to Schalau, the most common tomato disease in Arizona is the Curly Top Virus (CTV). This virus is spread by the beet leafhopper, and occurs most often in the early spring and usually happens after a wet fall and winter that creates many weeds in the desert. This makes for a good host environment for the leafhopper. The disease severely stunts the plant and eventually kills it; therefore, plants infected with CTV should be removed when identified.

With respect to his climate, Schalau said that at above 3,000 feet, Arizona's temperatures are relatively high, but not so high as to preclude fruiting. The good thing about the temperature in these areas is it makes for very few insect pests. At Arizona's lower elevations, tomato production ceases during the hottest months of June, July, and August. On the other hand, parts of Arizona pose different challenges. According to Schalau, "Late and early spring freezes are not unusual in the higher elevations (above 5,000 feet) of Arizona."

Some things about growing tomatoes are common across the country. Like most areas, the most common soil testing in Arizona is probably pH. This is particularly important for growing tomatoes. And like most areas, the most common deficiencies found in soils, when trying to grow tomatoes, are nitrogen and phosphorous.

Soil Requirements and Preparation

What is soil?

Soil can be defined as a combination of rock particles, air, water, and organic matter. Typical soil will have 45 percent rocks, 25 percent air, 25 percent water, and 5 percent organic matter. Rock particles are the primary component of soil and have been broken down over time by erosion into different size particles. These particles can be characterized into three broad types: sand, silt, and clay. Soil types then are typically described by the amount of sand, silt, or clay in the soil.

Sand: Of these components, sand has the largest particle size, so it has a rough texture. Soil containing large quantities of sand will not hold on well to water or nutrients.

Silt: Silt is composed of even smaller particles of disintegrated rocks. These particles tend to feel smooth and powdery to the touch and are easily eroded and carried away by wind or water. When wet, it feels smooth, but not sticky.

Clay: Clay is the smallest of soil particles. Like silt, it is smooth when dry, but when wet, clay becomes sticky. As a result, clay soil will hold on aggressively to water and nutrients. Too much clay creates a situation where particles stick together and, when dried, the soil becomes hard and firm. This prevents water and air from effectively entering the soil.

Loamy soil: Loamy soil is generally the target for all gardeners. Loam soil has a combination of sand, silt, and clay, with roughly a 40/40/20 percent distribution. This distribution tends to maximize the benefits and minimize the deficiencies of each of the individual components. Loamy soil retains nutrients well, but still allows water to flow adequately. These soils feel soft and crumble readily when dry, which makes them easy to till and work.

While organic matter represents a small portion of the components of the soil, it is the medium that provides nutrients that support plant growth. It also buffers the soil pH to keep acidity and alkalinity in check. Sand, silt, and clay are essentially used for structural support and as a medium to contain nutrients. Organic matter can come from many sources. In the woods, the majority of organic matter comes from dead leaves. In garden soil used year after year, organic matter is depleted by plant growth and must be replaced from year to year.

Improving the soil

While tomatoes can grow in almost any soil, the target soil for a tomato grower is loamy. The structure of soil in your own garden is not best determined by a soil test, but by the feel of the soil in your hands. As a guideline, a loamy, desirable soil can be formed into a ball that can easily be crumbled when moist. If a ball is difficult or impossible to form, the soil is sandy. If a ball is easily formed, but difficult to crumble, the soil is rich in clay. Another common technique used to diagnose your current soil structure is attempting to squeeze the moist soil into a ribbon. If your soil is predominately clay, you will be able to create a ribbon of several inches. If it is too sandy, you cannot create a ribbon of more than a half-inch or so. Few gardeners are blessed with perfect soil. The most common soil in tomato gardens has too much clay. Based on the above description of soil, the intuitive but wrong approach would be to add sand to these predominately clay soils. The problem is that to replace 50 percent of the soil with sand is generally prohibitively difficult. Furthermore, adding an insufficient quantity of sand can actually make the soil more dense and concrete-like when it dries.

Adding organic matter improves the texture of all soils. This matter can come in an array of forms, including ground corn husks, shredded leaves, lawn clippings, horse or cow manure, peat moss, or compost. Adding organic matter is never a permanent solution, as the matter will decay over time and will be absorbed by the plants or carried off with water drainage. Adding organic matter must be repeated year after year to maintain high quality, well-draining soil.

Important soil amendments

A soil amendment is any material added to a soil to improve its physical properties, such as water retention, permeability, water infiltration, drainage, aeration, and structure. While any list of amendments will automatically be incomplete, the following materials are generally reasonably easy to find and good for modifying soil structure and providing nutrients. For most soils, the most successful amendments are organic. The following organic amendments are popular:

Peat moss: Peat moss is the partial remains of sphagnum moss, which is found around ponds or in swamps or bogs. For the United States, peat moss is mostly harvested from Canadian bogs. Peat moss tends to increase the moisture, retaining characteristics and ease of cultivation of the soil. It will tend to make the soil somewhat more acidic.

Ground wood chips or sawdust: Adding wood to the soil tends to create an initial demand for nitrogen, as bacteria begins the decomposition process of the wood. As the wood decomposes, nitrogen is released and is again available for plants. As a result, some recommend adding a nitrogen-based fertilizer when adding wood to the garden, or adding the wood chips at least several months before you intend to plant, or even in the fall at the end of the garden season.

Manure: Fresh manure can be toxic to plants, due to high ammonia levels, so only aged manure (more than six months old) should be used in gardens. Manure from pets or other meat-eating animals should not be used for vegetable gardening soil because there is some risk of parasites or other disease-causing organisms being transmitted to humans. Manure, usually cow or horse, can usually be purchased from local farms or bought at garden supply stores. Composted manures provide a good source of nitrogen, potassium, and phosphorous.

Grass clippings: Grass clippings are an easy and usually readily available organic amendment. Clippings tend to degrade quickly to produce available nitrogen as nutrients. Grass clippings sometimes add weed seeds that can be problematic unless the clippings are well composted. Clippings should not be used if herbicides have recently been used on the grass.

Compost: Simply described, compost is the end product of the decomposition of organic matter. Therefore, composts can vary greatly in nutrients and structure with different starting materials and with the degree of degradation. Composts generally improve soil structure and drainage, and tend to make the soil easier to cultivate. *For more information on composting, see Chapter 9.*

Leaves or straw: Shred leaves or straw before using as a soil amendment in order to speed up the decomposition process and maximize impact on soil structure and nutrients. These materials are fibrous and are an excellent amendment for soils that are clay-rich, as they improve porosity, aeration, and drainage. You can add pine straw to tomato gardens, but over time it will increase the acidity of the soil.

Wood ash: If you have a natural supply of wood ash, you can use this as a garden amendment. Wood ash tends to increase the pH of the soil and also tends to contain a fair amount of potassium. Depending on your native soil composition, this could be good or bad for your soil. Most wood types are fine, although walnut wood ash is known to have some toxins that are dangerous for garden vegetable plants.

A few amendments are inorganic, and these amendments do not supply any nutrients to the soil. They can, in the right circumstances, serve to improve the structure and drainage characteristics of the soil. These amendments include the following:

Vermiculite: Vermiculite is a natural mineral with a clay structure. When superheated, it expands and forms small light particles that can improve soil structure. It is recognized as the small, white, very lightweight particles that look like Styrofoam and is often found in potting soils. As it is a type of clay, it increases the water-holding properties of soil, so it is useful as an additive to sandy soils. Vermiculite should not be added to clay soils. Vermiculite has become somewhat difficult to locate as a soil amendment, as the major mine for the United States in Montana was contaminated with asbestos and was closed in the 1990s. As a result, vermiculite is mostly mined in South Africa or Brazil and can be somewhat expensive to use.

Perlite: Perlite is a volcanic rock that also expands greatly when superheated. It is easily recognized in many purchased soil mixes as it is the small, lightweight, white particles that have the feel of Styrofoam. It is generally used to reduce soil density and will help improve soil aeration and reduce compaction.

Chapter 4:
Starting Tomatoes from Seed

While this chapter will describe a number of practical benefits derived from starting tomato plants from seed, for the home gardener, there is one psychological benefit that may outweigh all the more analytical ones. Starting seeds inside on a cold, dreary winter day is a statement of hope and optimism that spring and a breath of new life is coming. It is the pre-season game, for which the planning begins in January or February, with the first perusal of seed catalogues or Web sites.

Benefits of Starting From Seed

Tomatoes are one of the vegetable crops where you benefit most from starting plants from seed indoors because they tolerate transplanting exceptionally well. Even in areas where it is warm enough to start tomato seeds directly in the garden, it is often advised to start seeds inside. This will provide controlled conditions to increase germination rate and will better limit exposing fragile seedlings to unexpected weather or pathogens.

However, the decision to buy plants or seeds also depends a lot on your own personal constraints around weather, time, and space. Seedlings can require daily attention to adjust lighting, fertilizing, and water; so if you have significant travel plans during this period or you are only planting a small number of plants, buying tomato plants may be your best option.

Economy

Starting your tomato plants from seed is almost always the low-cost approach for growing tomatoes. If you are happy with some of the most popular standard tomato varieties, tomato seeds can be found in local discount stores for prices as low as 20 seeds for a dollar. Germination rates are high and if you are creative and conservative in finding and reusing starting containers, you can have plants in the garden for 10 to 20 cents per plant. Even purchasing seeds from nurseries or online seed suppliers — where many more varieties are available — will be significantly more economical than buying or ordering plants. With starting seeds indoors, there is also an economy of scale. If you only want two or three tomato plants, you probably will not recognize much savings. However, if you are planting a large variety of plants and have freezing or canning in your plans, you will save a good deal of money and generally have extra plants you can share with friends. *A list of catalogs, online stores, and physical locations where you can purchase tomato seeds is included in Appendix A.*

Selection

You will have a much more extensive array of options for tomato plant varieties to grow in your garden if you choose to start your tomato plants from seed rather than buying transplants. This may be the most meaningful advantage to you. Multiple Web sites offer more than 500 different hybrid and heirloom tomato varieties, with new ones available every year.

Quality control/timing

Starting your own seeds also gives you control over the seed selection and germination process that can help you ensure high quality, disease-free seedlings. As you always start more seeds than you plan to plant in the garden, you will almost always have extra seedlings from which you can choose the strongest and healthiest plants. Also, if you are constrained to buying plants in local stores and your timing is not good, you could be relegated to picking from crowded, spindly plants that will be less likely to survive the garden. Starting tomatoes yourself from seed gives you the most flexibility in timing your plants, so you can have healthy plants with a strong root system once the planting time has arrived in your area.

Equipment Options

Flats and trays

There is an extensive array of containers designed and sold for starting vegetable seeds for the garden. It is also likely that you have a number of container options around the house that would do well for this purpose. Many gardeners prefer to plant seeds together in flats or trays rather than individual pots initially. While germination rates are typically very high for most varieties of tomato seeds, the rates will vary from year to year. Planting in trays with seeds roughly 3/4 of an inch apart, gives you the capability to easily separate and transplant individual seedlings without disturbing their neighbors, even when 100 percent of seeds germinate. Trays that are roughly 3 to 4 inches deep are ideal. Several smaller trays are more convenient than one larger tray, as this allows you to more carefully organize and keep a number of different varieties of tomatoes separate. It also makes it easy to manage once the seedlings germinate and you begin to expose them to light. It is best to use planting trays with small drainage holes in the bottom to avoid overwatering the seeds. Recycling containers from year to year is a good idea; just be sure to clean them well from season to season, as some fungi and molds are hardy and could survive over the winter.

Planting medium

Potting soil is typically not the medium of choice for starting tomato seeds. Potting soil tends to be heavier with larger particles and more variable consistency. While more mature plants will need potting soil for support of heavy plants, seedlings will be more successful in a finer medium that provides more uniform moisture, is free from weed seeds, and does not have large particles that can obstruct a germinating seed. Most nurseries or discount stores sell soil-starting mix. You can also mix up your own seed medium, which is a more economical solution.

Tomato Tidbits

A standard recipe for making your own planting medium is to mix one part sphagnum peat moss and one part perlite or vermiculite. Fertilizer or compost is never added to seed medium before seeds germinate, as the concentrated nitrogen may damage seeds.

For the most frugal gardener, there is an additional option. If you have reasonably loamy garden soil, it is possible to filter the soil and then bake it for roughly 45 minutes at 180 degrees Fahrenheit. Filtering the soil takes out any larger rocks or particles in the garden soil, and the baking will serve to sterilize the soil to clear it of any fungal or bacterial disease organisms that might have persisted over the winter.

A compromise option is to use sterilized garden soil for the bottom half of the seedling tray and seed starter mix for the top half.

"Damping off" is a somewhat generic term used to describe reduced germination and/or thin stalks that develop just above the medium surface and cause the seedlings to fall over and die. Damping off can be caused by a variety of different fungi, and the primary way to prevent it is by using the right soilless medium for seed germination.

Watering tools

Pouring water from a pitcher directly on newly seeded medium or newly germinated seeds can be problematic. Seed medium is by design lighter than potting soil, and can easily be washed away from soils or seedlings. An easy watering system for germinating seeds is a clean kitchen plastic spray bottle. These are often found in seed catalogs or discount stores, but standard kitchen cleaner spray bottles can also be washed thoroughly and recycled as seedling spray bottles. This provides a nice mist that avoids disturbing the planting medium or the developing root system of the seeding. Another alternative is the old-fashioned watering can with the long spout and a fine grating on the end, which disrupts the stream of water.

Lights

While tomato seeds do not require light to germinate, they will need light once they do germinate. The simplest and least expensive option is to find a southern-facing window that gets steady sunlight, and set up a stand for tomato seedlings next to this window. However, the position of this window is not always convenient, and bright sunlight is not always a consistent commodity in winter months. In addition, using window light will require rotation of the seedling trays or pots to prevent the plants from leaning into the sun. Fluorescent lighting tends to be a much more reliable method for ensuring consistently adequate lighting for your seedlings. With fluorescent lighting, tomato seedlings can be set up in a variety of locations in your home with electric timers to turn them on and off. Nurseries and online garden sites will also offer special gardening grow lights, but these tend to be more expensive. Also, there is little evidence these bulbs produce better tomato plant growth than much cheaper standard fluorescent bulbs for plants less than 10 to 12 inches tall.

As tomato seedlings will grow rapidly, it is best to set up tomato seedlings on a stand or shelf. As the plants begin to grow taller, you should be able to adjust the distance of the light from the top of the tomato plants. Various approaches will work for setting this up. Building a frame from polyvinyl chloride (PVC) plumbing tubing and connectors is simple and economical option. A fluorescent bulb housing with two fluorescent bulbs suspended with chains is usually included with the purchased bulb housing. This can be adjusted for several sizes of flats and the chains can be easily adjusted to change the height of the fluorescent light continuously as the seedlings grow taller. The PVC pipes can be glued with solvent to make a permanent frame or can just be slipped into place so that it can be disassembled after use and easily stored away.

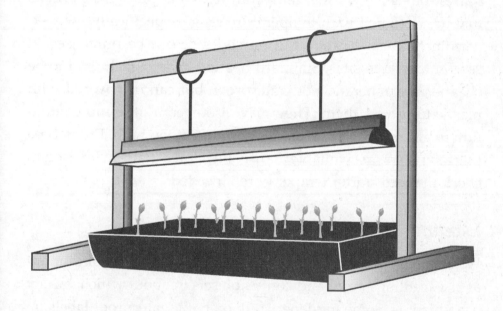

DIAGRAM 4: SEEDLING LIGHT STAND

For larger quantities of seedlings, a shelving system can be the best option. Assemble several shelves with fluorescent bulbs attached to the bottom of each shelf for the plants on the next lower shelf. You can adjust plant height by changing the height of the shelves or by putting the seedling flats on blocks and removing the blocks as they grow. However you set up your lights, adding a reflective shield made from strips of heavy duty aluminum foil over and around the plants is a good idea to maximize the light from the fluorescent bulbs and to help get adequate light to lower level foliage.

Heating pads

While typical indoor winter temperatures are probably conducive for good tomato plant growth, tomato seed germination requires somewhat warmer temperatures. Waterproof heated mats that are designed with temperature ranges specifically for seed germination can be found in nurseries or can be purchased at seed source Web sites. Standard heating pads, which tend to be cheaper, are generally not waterproof, but can be covered with plastic to protect them. They may also need a little more attention to ensure the temperature does not get too high. Probe-type thermometers are available at discount stores that can be used to check the seed starter temperature if needed.

Labeling

While labeling seems like a trivial matter, it becomes important as the seedlings grow and confusion sets in about which variety each plant is. Some gardeners rely on both waterproof labels on the outside of the seedling tray and on a logbook that diagrams what, where, and when seedlings have been planted. Another option is to use waterproof white label stakes purchased at garden supply stores.

CASE STUDY: DAVIS AND DORCUS WEBB REMEMBER GARDENS OF THE PAST

Davis and Dorcus Webb
Long-time home gardeners
Oakwood, Georgia

The Webbs both grew up in the 1930s and 40s growing and enjoying tomatoes. They share some of their recollections from gardening over the years.

Davis and Dorcus Webb have been growing tomatoes in their families for as long as they can remember. Dorcus was born in 1931 in rural South Georgia on a family farm. South Georgia has good soil and a great climate for tomatoes. Dorcus's family grew field crops — such as corn and peanuts — for the farm. They also grew vegetables — including many tomatoes — in the family garden. "There were 12 children in the family and we typically planted probably 200 tomato plants each year," Dorcus said. She remembers that her family grew a tomato plant with a shorter, bushier structure that they didn't need to stake. "Dad used to dry and save tomato seeds to plant the next season," Dorcus said. They didn't have any problem with wildlife bothering the tomato garden because they raised livestock, so they had a good fence all around the family garden to protect it. The stock ran free, but the tomatoes were fenced in.

Davis was born in 1929 and was more a city boy, growing up in Atlanta. Nonetheless, his family still had a vegetable garden and grew tomatoes. He and his brothers also spent the summers with their grandparents working on the farm. "We were sort of itinerant farm labor," Davis said. He continues to grow tomatoes today, typically buying transplants for planting and tending to stick with the classics. Davis's family tended to plant Rutgers, Park's Whopper, Marglobes, and Better Boys, and liked to plant varieties with as much disease resistance as possible.

Like most long-time growers, Davis and Dorcus have their own formulas for success. "We mix composted leaves, potting soil, a couple of table-spoons of 10-10-10 fertilizer, and some Epsom salts, then place this mixture in the bottom of each hole. We like to cut off the bottom leaves and place plants deep in the hole. This promotes more root growth —

the more roots you have, the more tomatoes you will pick," Davis said. The Webbs dig a small hole about the size of a coffee cup about 6 inches from each plant and put fertilizer in these holes about every two weeks. They also add fireplace ash and banana and potato peelings directly to the garden.

Both of the Webbs eat tomatoes regularly, but Dorcus is probably the bigger fan. "When I was young, we ate tomatoes year-round," Dorcus said. "Tomato sandwiches in the summer were my favorite. And we used tomatoes that we had canned for the winter to make rice and tomatoes, Brunswick stew, okra and tomatoes, vegetable soup, and eggs with tomato gravy. We ate so many tomatoes back then that my dad used to say our blood was probably 100 percent tomato juice."

Seed Starting

Timing for starting seeds

If you are like most gardeners, your primary timing objective is getting ripe tomatoes as early in the summer as possible. If this is your objective, the best rule of thumb is to start tomato seeds six weeks before the date of the average last spring frost in your area. As the target date for planting seedlings into the garden is two weeks after this average last spring frost, starting seeds at six weeks before will make them eight weeks old when planted in the garden. Do not be tempted to start seeds any earlier than eight weeks before this date, as your tomato plants will be larger when they are transplanted into the garden. They will not grow as quickly as younger, smaller transplants. The last spring frost date can vary by as much as a month from year to year, so be prepared to adjust your planting date if the spring is particularly warm, cold, or rainy. Information can vary somewhat from source to source, as some use different definitions for calculating the averages. Also, it is important to distinguish between a freeze, which is explicitly defined as when the temperature reaches 32 degrees Fahrenheit, and a frost, which can occur at temperatures up to 36 to 38 degrees Fahrenheit depending on humidity, elevation, and dew point. Tomato seedlings are fairly fragile and can be damaged or destroyed by frost, which occurs at these higher temperatures.

There are several Internet sites that give information about last spring frost dates in your area. The National Climatic Data Center (**www.ncdc.noaa.gov**) is the best resource for this information; providing data for freeze points as well as for temperatures several degrees above and below the freeze point. Another Internet-based option, which includes information on past data for spring frosts and predictions for future springs, is the Mother Earth News Web (**www.motherearthnews.com**). Additionally, *The Farmers' Almanac*, a book published annually since 1818, has an excellent Web site to guide your gardening habits. Visit **www.farmersalmanac.com** and click "Home & Garden." Another even more reliable resource may be your local agricultural extension service, as their information will be tailored to your specific area and include micro-climates that may impact your planting dates.

In some situations, having the earliest ripening tomatoes from your plants may not be your primary objective. You may be looking for a later ripening date to accommodate personal travel plans, garden festivals, or other special events. In this case, you should consult the seed package or seed vendor where the days from transplant to ripe fruit will be listed on the package or in the product description. As previously mentioned, days from transplant to harvest for tomatoes range from roughly 55 to 85 days. This will, of course, depend on water, light, and soil conditions, and can vary by several weeks on either side of the target date.

Nonetheless, the days from transplant to harvest can be added to the roughly 56 days from seed to transplant to allow you to back-calculate from a special event to a planted seed date. Personal extended summer travel or vacation plans should especially be considered when planting determinate varieties. As described before, the fruit on a determinate tomato variety will all ripen at approximately the same time over a narrow time window of about two weeks. If summer travel and determinate tomatoes are both in your plans, consider the timing of your planting so you can limit overlap.

Quantity of seeds

A safe and conservative assumption is that 50 percent of your seeds will not germinate or survive transplanting. Most experience a good deal better than 50 percent germination rate and some see germination rates as high as 95 percent. However, as seeds are generally reasonably inexpensive and timing is important, it is better to err on the side of the conservative, especially in your early gardening years. Tomato seeds tend to come in packets of 20 to 30 seeds. For a small- to medium-sized garden, buying and starting seeds will almost always result in some leftover seeds. Smaller packets tend to cost more per seed, so the more economical approach is buying the bigger packet and saving seeds for the next season. You can successfully save seeds for the next year — often for several years — with some reduction in germination rate as they age. Tomato seeds will survive for several years in a dry, cool, dark environment. There is actually documented evidence of 50-year-old seeds, carefully stored, that germinated. While this survival rate is by no means common, the average gardener can certainly save extra seeds for two to three years and avoid repurchasing the next year. A good option is to put different seed varieties in small, labeled envelopes bundled together in a glass jar. It is wise to include a desiccant (a drying agent) in the jar, to help keep the air surrounding the seeds dry. Desiccants can be reclaimed from a variety of consumer-packaged products. They are the small, often white, packages that usually say "Do Not Eat." As an alternative, fresh powdered milk in a cloth bag can also be used a desiccant.

Planting seeds

Mix medium and add it to seed trays. Add water to the medium and mix it well. Water does not spread out on or absorb into a seeding medium as quickly as it does with soil, so you should give the planting medium several hours to equilibrate. It should be uniformly moist when seeds are added. Add water until the medium is moist, but not saturated, similar to a squeezed sponge. Seeds should be planted to ¼ inch deep, roughly 1 inch apart. A standard technique is poking holes in the medium with an unsharpened pencil and then covering with additional medium. If you are planting multiple varieties of tomatoes or other vegetables, careful labeling is critical because seedlings will often be impossible to identify. A garden log is also a good idea to help keep track of planting dates and seed varieties. The logbook will also give you more data from which to make good decisions as you adjust garden choices for the next season's plantings. Cover the seed trays with a piece of moisture-proof kitchen plastic wrap to keep the medium from drying out, but leave one end open to provide some air circulation and lessen the chances of fungus or mold growth. This air circulation is another step to help avoid damping off. This basically creates a mini-greenhouse for your seeds and seedlings early days. *For a sample of a garden log, see Appendix D.*

Watering

With the seed flats moistened well and covered with plastic wrap, the seed medium should stay moist until the seeds germinate. If they need to be watered, it is a good idea to use water that is warmed up to a temperature of about 75 degrees Fahrenheit, especially if your home is cool in the winter. Once the seeds have germinated and the seedlings start to grow, remove the plastic wrap and ensure that your seedling trays are watered regularly, as the seedlings have minimal root structure at this point. Water until the medium is very moist and then let the seed medium surface get just barely dry before watering again. Never let seedlings wilt or become limp due to a shortage of water. This could mean watering about every other day under some conditions. Water carefully with a sprayer or a fine-mist watering can to avoid washing away the new fragile seedlings. Again, especially if the location is cooler than 65 degrees Fahrenheit, it is a good idea to warm the water up to 75 degree Fahrenheit to encourage faster germination.

Light and temperature

While some vegetable seeds, such as lettuce, require light to germinate, tomatoes do not. Warmth, however, is required. Tomato seeds will germinate at temperatures as low as 50 degrees Fahrenheit, but germination will be faster with a higher percentage of seeds germinating when the temperature is maintained between 70 and 80 degrees Fahrenheit. As seeds may be started indoors in some areas as early as January or February, it is unlikely that indoor temperatures will be this high. Some recommend putting seed trays on top of a refrigerator or over a fireplace mantle to help with keeping the seed medium warm. Another good — and probably more reliable — option is to place seed trays on heated mats as previously described.

Tomato seeds kept moist at 70 to 80 degrees Fahrenheit will usually germinate in five to eight days. Once the seeds have germinated, they need to be moved quickly into a lighted area. Seedlings that are kept in low light will quickly grow tall and leggy and begin to lean aggressively into the light. When using fluorescent lights, tomato seedlings should be under the lights for 16 to 18 hours per day. A timer is invaluable as a worry-free method to make sure that new seedlings get reliable and ample light.

Seedlings will do well with soil temperatures from 60 to 80 degrees Fahrenheit. Stem and foliage growth will be more rapid at temperatures on the higher end of this range. If the soil or air temperature is too high, the plants will become too tall and leggy.

Fertilizing

The first pair of leaves that germinate in tomatoes are not actually true leaves, but are called 'cotyledons' — these are the energy reservoirs for the seeds. Typically, tomatoes are bicotyledons, but there are a few varieties that have three cotyledons. Several days after new seedlings have germinated, it is time to begin adding a weak fertilizer to the seedling tray. Water-soluble fertilizers should be diluted to roughly 25 percent of the normal recommended dilution. Add this fertilizer solution in place of water about once per week. The first true leaves on the seedling appear between the two cotyledons, and they will resemble mature tomato plant leaves.

Potting Up and Hardening Off

Once one or two sets of true leaves have developed on the seedlings, it is time to transplant seedlings into individual pots or into individual sections of divided trays. Containers should be around 2 to 4 inches wide. There are a variety of containers available in garden supply stores or discount stores. Small Styrofoam cups with small holes poked in the bottom will also work fine for home gardeners. The typical recommendation is to continue to use a soilless transplant medium, although, at this point it is not as critical as during the seed germination stage. Be very careful with seedlings, as they are very fragile. Attempt to handle seedlings by the leaves rather than by the stems because the stem can be easily damaged and would destroy the entire plant. If any seedlings end up too close together in your flats, it is better to sacrifice one by snipping off the top with small scissors rather than trying to disentangle the thin seedling roots. Use a small spoon to lift the seedlings below the root structure to move into the new container. Set the seedling deep into the new container with the cotyledons just above the surface of the medium to encourage more root growth. Continue to water and fertilize with dilute solution and regularly adjust the height to keep the fluorescent lights no more than 2 to 3 inches above the top of the plants.

Hardening off is the process of gradually introducing your pampered seedlings into the outdoors. Plants grown inside have not been exposed to wind, fluctuating temperatures, or direct sunlight. Full sunlight, cool temperatures, or a combination of both can shock transplants if exposed to these conditions too abruptly. About ten to 14 days before the target date for planting outdoors, begin to move plants outside for short but increasing periods of time during the day, ideally during the warmest part of the afternoon. Initially put plants in a partial shady area protected from the wind and gradually move into more sunny areas. Bring plants back inside well before dark. By the end of the two weeks, plants can stay outside in sunny areas in the day and throughout the night, if there is no frost or wind in the forecast.

Seed starting summary

- Use a soilless seed starting mix and moisten it thoroughly at least an hour before planting.

- Start seeds about eight weeks before you want to plant outdoors.

- Cover the planted seeds to maintain moisture, leaving a little room for air circulation.

- Place in a warm spot to achieve a seed temperature of about 75 degrees Fahrenheit.

- As soon as seeds germinate, remove cover and place under lights for 16 hours per day.

- Water regularly to keep medium moist.

- Feed with weak fertilizer once per week.

- Transplant into individual units when one or two sets of true leaves appear.

- Move outside during the day to harden off a few days before planting outside.

- Plant.

Chapter 5:
Planting Outside

Timing

The decision about timing for transplanting tomato plants into the garden is, of course, primarily driven by geography and local climate. In the semi-tropical weather of South Florida, where winter frosts are rare, it is possible to begin planting tomatoes in late August and continue planting them until March. This planting schedule will deliver a harvest beginning in November and continuing until late June or July. On the other hand, in some parts of Maine — where the average last frost date is June 1 — a gardener will be challenged to reliably get tomato plants in the garden before June begins and will be happy to get tomatoes in early August.

Tomatoes are very susceptible to frost damage, so they should always be planted outside after all danger of frost has passed. Check the historical data on average and last spring frost dates for your area and use them as a guide. The average last frost date generally refers to the date with a 50/50 chance of frost after this date, so planting on this date definitely carries a good deal of risk. The date for no chance of frost is generally around two weeks after the average last frost date. A good rule of thumb is to target for having plants hardened off and ready to go in the ground about two weeks after the average last frost date. In some years, you will easily plant at this time. In other cooler years, you may need to continue the hardening off process for another week.

While it is tempting to try and aggressively reach as early a planting date as is possible, planting tomatoes early generally offers few rewards. While an early cool weather planting may miss a killing frost, tomato plants will not start to grow actively until the ground temperature reaches at least 50 degrees Fahrenheit. Warm ground temperature is in fact more important to early tomato plant growth performance than is warm air temperature. Some gardeners even use temperature probes to check soil temperatures for more confidence in planting dates. Because soil warmth is more important to plant growth than just the lack of frost, it is not unusual for the eager gardener to get his tomato plants in the ground two weeks before his less anxious neighbor, but still not yield ripe tomatoes any earlier. Tomato plants may survive some cool spring nights, but essentially they will rest dormant until the soil is sufficiently warm.

On the other hand, planting tomatoes too late — particularly in areas in the southern United States — is problematic as well. The phase of growth when flowers turn into fruit is called "fruit set," and hot summer temperatures will inhibit fruit set in tomatoes.

The optimum temperature for fruit set for the tomato is between 65 and 80 degrees Fahrenheit. At above 90 degrees Fahrenheit, the fruit set will become very limited. For this reason, seed planting and/or transplanting into the garden must be timed so the plant is not flowering during the hottest part of the summer.

Another consideration is the timing of spring rains. Occasionally, while temperatures may have become sufficiently warm, spring rains may be frequent and plentiful enough to keep the garden too wet for planting. Again, the race is not always to be the fastest in this situation. It is better to be patient and wait for the soil to be dry enough to work easily. Working with soil that is too moist will tend to compact it around the plant and reduce drainage and aeration.

Finally, transplant tomato plants to the garden on a cloudy day or later in the afternoon after the sun is no longer at its peak or where your garden has a little shade. Fresh tomato transplants are just as often damaged by sunburn as they are by cold weather.

CASE STUDY: MASTER GARDENER SHARES TIPS

Ray Stern
Master Gardener
Cumming, Georgia

Ray Stern is a scientist, a long-time gardener, and a master gardener in Forsyth County, Georgia. He has been growing tomatoes for 25 years and in keeping with his scientific training, regularly experiments in his garden with new vegetable varieties and new approaches. He shares his favorite tomato tips.

Like many gardeners, Stern comes from a family of gardeners, so he has relied partly on his father's experience for guidance in gardening. His own experience has also given him additional guidance. Because Stern has gardened in Georgia for many years, he has had time to refine his choice of tomato varieties to those that flourish in his local soil and climate.

"My father loves the Celebrity tomato, and it really does well for him in Texas," Stern said. "In Georgia, I have never gotten more than six tomatoes per vine. My favorite tomato to grow is probably the Juliet. I bought it because it was advertised as a grape tomato and I was expecting small grape-sized tomatoes. What I got was medium-sized, pear-shaped tomatoes, like Roma but indeterminate. It is an aggressive grower that will completely cover a 12-foot-long, 6-foot-high trellis, and each vine produces several bushels of tomatoes. Three or four vines will produce enough tomatoes to make sauce and canned tomatoes for our family for an entire year. They are also perfect snack size and have a sweet but still-tangy taste."

Stern's experience with tomatoes also illustrates the maxim "Theory guides. Experiment decides." Gardening experts almost universally recommend crop rotation for tomatoes. However, while rotation certainly mitigates the risk of disease, sometimes it is just not practical. Although he knows crop rotation is recommended for tomatoes, he just cannot rotate tomatoes to areas of the garden where they have never grown before — mostly because he uses raised beds with permanent trellises and trains the tomatoes onto the trellis. In this way, tomatoes grow in the same area every year. Also, he composts his vines every year and spreads the compost over the entire garden, so varieties with disease-resistance are important. "It really is survival of the fittest in my garden," Stern said.

In Georgia, Stern adds, the growing season is so long that it makes no sense to rush tomatoes into the ground. They will not start growing until the soil warms up anyway. He does not worry about frost protection early in the season because he waits until a couple weeks after the last frost date until setting out transplants. In his area, he also prefers indeterminates over determinates. Indeterminates make better use of the gardening space. When determinates quit producing, it is a bad time in the season to replant anything else in that area.

The Buying Tomato Plants Option

Not everyone is interested in starting tomatoes from seed and managing seedlings until transplant time. When you are only planting a few tomato plants — about six or less — there is less advantage from an economic or variety perspective. In addition, raising healthy seedlings can be a demand on your time and will certainly be a challenge if travel or work prevents you from being around to monitor and tend to fledgling seedlings at least every other day or so. All the steps in watering, fertilizing, adjusting lights, re-potting, and hardening off do not have to be extremely time intensive, but they do demand some attention on a fairly frequent and regular basis.

So, for a number of reasons, the best option for your tomato garden may be to purchase tomato plants for transplanting. The ideal tomato plant for planting in the garden is 8 to 12 inches tall with a dark green color and healthy-looking foliage. If the objective is productivity and yield, it is generally not best to use plants that have already begun to flower or that already have small green fruit. Generally, tomatoes go through several phases of growth, from seedling growth to rapid foliage and stem growth to a reproductive phase. If you choose transplants that have already entered the reproductive phase, your plants may produce the earliest ripe fruit but early harvest will likely come at a price. Plants that are in the reproductive phase when they are transplanted will not tend to grow as large and will not likely set as many blossoms as healthy — but smaller — transplants. Smaller transplants will have time to grow stronger stems and more lush foliage and will ultimately result in more blossoms and more fruit. Also, a larger plant will be better able to resist disease and weather challenges than a smaller plant with a fruit production out of proportion to its size.

In the spring, healthy tomato plants can be purchased locally from nurseries, garden centers, home improvement stores, and big discount stores. Locally appropriate varieties can also often be found at farmers' markets or local farming stands. If you are in search of more exotic varieties, a number of companies offer catalogue or Internet-based shipping options for hybrid or heirloom tomatoes. Also, with the popularity of home tomato growing, it is not unusual to have friends or neighbors who start tomato seedlings indoors and generally always have extras to share. *An extensive list of resources is included in Appendix A.*

Spacing, Depth, and Placement

It is finally time to put those pampered transplants into your carefully prepared garden. The minimum distance you should put between plants is dependent on the type of support structure you have planned and also on the type of tomato you are planting. Spacing can vary from as little as 1 foot between plants for some dwarf and other small determinate varieties. Tomatoes that are staked and tied carefully to posts can also be spaced as little as 1 foot apart. Caged plants are typically spaced farther apart and should be at least 2 feet apart. For tomatoes that you allow to sprawl with support, at least 3 feet should be allowed between each plant. It is good to allow at least 3 feet between tomato rows, primarily to allow room for weeding and working on the plants.

These distances are generally thought of as minimums. Basically, there are only advantages to giving the tomatoes even more space if space is available in the garden. Both indeterminate tomato plants — with their long, sprawling vines — as well as shorter — but more bushy and thick — determinate varieties will appreciate the extra space. A healthy amount of space between plants and rows will give room to use power equipment for tilling or mowing between the rows. Root structures will thrive more successfully if given plenty of room to spread and seek moisture and nutrients. For well-established plants, tomato root structures can spread laterally across 5 feet or more. Also, close spacing of plants can limit sunlight to lower foliage and compromise growth. Especially if the objective is more tomatoes, allowing extra space between plants will contribute to more successful results.

Tomato plants should always be planted at least 2 inches deeper in the garden soil than in their current temporary containers. This is because tomato vines have what botanists call "adventitious stems," meaning that new root structures will develop from the surface of the tomato plant stem. The taller the transplants are, the deeper they should be planted in the garden. Deeper planting will lead to the development of a deeper and more stable root structure; therefore, you will yield stronger plants. Field experiments have shown that planting at the same depth as the original transplant leads to both smaller and fewer fruits.

Some gardeners take even more aggressive advantage of this adventitious rooting by laying their transplants on their sides during the hardening off period. This forces the tomato plants to grow stems that curve up toward the sun. After four to five days of growing like this, the plants will have formed a nice, almost 90-degree curve. Trenches — rather than holes — are then dug in the garden and the root ball and plant are placed in the trench so the end of the plant curves up and out of the end of the trench. This provides for a lot of stem surface area that forms additional adventitious roots.

When transplants are particularly long and leggy, burying plants deep is even more important. In this case, put plants at least 3 inches below the level of the soil or use the trenching method described above. If you feel like root growth needs a little extra encouragement, you can also remove the first set of true leaves and plant these below the surface. The extra root system, — and the stability and nutrients that it will provide — will more than make up for the loss of a few inches of top stem growth that you are giving away. Also, if your transplants have matured to the point of blooming or having fruit, snip off the fruit or flowers before planting them in your garden.

Garden soil should be broadcast fertilized and tilled several days before the tomato plants are planted. Unless your soil test results are particularly unbalanced or unusual, a standard recommendation for fertilizer before planting is 2 to 3 pounds of a balanced (10-10-10) fertilizer per 100 square feet of garden space. The soil should be sufficiently moist so it is easily worked without creating dust, but not so moist that is compacts and densifies readily. Dig holes for transplanting roughly 12 inches deep and about 12 to 18 inches wide, depending on the size of your transplant. You can never add too much organic matter with tomato plants, so use this as another opportunity to enrich the soil. A good guideline is to refill the hole with half soil and half organic matter; compost, leaves, peat moss, or aged manure. You can also mix a couple of tablespoons of balanced fertilizer into the hole.

Transplants should be watered thoroughly in their containers before moving them into the garden. The objective is to have the growing medium moist enough so it clings well to the root system and the plant can be transplanted with a root ball of medium attached to the plant. This contributes to the least trauma to the root system. If your tomato transplants were grown in peat pots, be sure to remove the rim of the peat pot or at least assure that the pot is below the surface of the soil as the exposed peat rim will tend to dry the root ball. After transplanting into the garden soil, the plant should be watered again to wash soil into air pockets around the roots and to assure that the root system stays moist. A best practice is to put some dry soil on top of the watered plants to keep a soil crust from forming on the top.

For growers who have a history of cutworm problems or are in an area where cutworms are prevalent, prevention during planting is the answer. Cutworms are the larvae of moths that last the winter in the soil and can destroy many young seedlings quickly by chewing through the stem at the soil line. As the plants get older and tougher, cutworms cease to be a threat. The easy solution is to slip the seedling though an open-ended cylinder or box that you can embed slightly in the ground and leave with roughly 2 inches exposed. This will create a collar around the seedling and prevent the cutworms from being able to reach the tomato stems. There are many creative options for creating cutworm collars, including empty toilet paper or paper towel rolls cut to size, as they are free and biodegradable. For larger transplants, you can also cut the bottom out of old used small plastic planters and slip these around the plant stem.

Growing Early Tomatoes

After a long cold winter without fresh tomatoes, the typical gardener is very anxious for fresh vine-ripe tomatoes, so early tomatoes often become one of the tomato garden objectives. Some gardeners who live in more northern climates with early fall frost dates need to focus on early tomatoes just to assure an adequate harvest. Following are some strategies for growing early tomatoes for either of these circumstances:

Starting seeds and transplanting for early tomatoes

Seeds for early variety tomatoes can be started about a week earlier than when you plant your regular season varieties. You can use this extra time to repot plants into larger containers to allow the root system to expand and develop more fully. Research has shown that using pots for transplants that are at least 2 ½ to 3 inches in diameter will help them develop a larger root system, bloom earlier, and produce earlier fruit. You should aim to put these early varieties in the ground at just about the last frost date, which will probably be a week or so earlier than your other tomatoes. Be prepared to adjust your planting date if the spring is unseasonably late and cool. It is also not a bad idea to stagger some of your plantings to provide some backup plants in case an unexpected cold snap kills or stunts your first try at planting in the garden. Even more than with regular tomatoes, a healthy dose of compost in the planting mix is important for ensuring that adequate nutrients are available.

Another approach that can work well for short season gardeners — as demonstrated in experimental trials — is to avoid any transplanting at all of the early varieties you start from seed. Seeds are planted directly into a 4-inch container and grown without transplanting until the plant and weather are ready for moving into the garden soil. The natural root structure of the tomato plant is a long deep taproot. Generally, transplanting disrupts or breaks this taproot, and a more fibrous and generally shallower root structure will develop. Trials have demonstrated that seedlings that were not transplanted one or two times prior to planting in the garden produced more and faster ripening fruit. Overall yields for these plants were all equivalent, so the transplanted plants essentially caught up eventually.

Tips and strategies for early tomatoes

Be vigilant about the weather forecast for cool nights for your early season tomatoes. Cardboard boxes or buckets can be used as covers at night to protect against frost. Popular frost covers are gallon-sized milk jugs with the bottom cut out of them. Remember that frost can occur at temperatures several degrees above freezing. Another option that might give you some additional advantage is using dark plastic film to cover the ground around the tomatoes. The black plastic will absorb additional heat during the day and help to warm the soil. Do not put the plastic close to the tomatoes; the plastic should allow space for adequate moisture and air to reach the root system. Other organic mulches can prevent the soil from warming up as quickly in the spring so if you want to use clippings, leaves, or straw, postpone putting these on until the soil temperature reaches at least 60 degrees Fahrenheit.

Root pruning is another approach often used for trying to push the ripening of early tomatoes by a few days or so. Use a spade or small shovel and slice down into the soil in a circle around the tomato plant stem to a depth of about 6 to 8 inches. The circle should be about 10 inches from the tomato stem. This will sever parts of the root system, which will encourage earlier ripening. The idea is that the stress to the plant, caused by cutting the roots, causes the plant to rush to complete its life cycle and produce fruit and seed. Root prune when the plant has several clusters of good-sized green fruit. Root pruning may reduce the overall season yield of the plant so you would not want to use this trick on all of your plants. On the other end of the spectrum, root pruning can also be used at the end of the season when you have green tomatoes still on your tomato vines and would like them to ripen before an anticipated frost. Weathermen jokes asides, in most areas a significant frost is often anticipated by four to five days, and this could potentially give you time to push some tomatoes to ripen.

 **Tomato Tidbits**

For the impatient who are anxious to push for the very earliest garden tomatoes, another idea is to dig out roughly half of the soil in one small section of your garden and replace it with sand. Mix it well and then plant a couple of early variety tomatoes in this sandy soil. Sandy soils warm much more quickly in the spring and will help the plant get a head start. Moisture will drain from this area quickly, so be sure to keep it well watered.

Several tactics that are good for any regular season tomatoes are even better for gardeners trying to push for the earliest season tomato. One of these is planting depth. For early season tomatoes, putting the plant into the garden soil at least up to the level of the first set of true leaves will contribute to ripening several days earlier. Another tactic important for all tomatoes — but particularly relevant for early season tomatoes — is to fertilize with a balanced fertilizer as soon as your plants begin to produce fruit. This extra dose of nutrients will support the energy demands of fruit production and ripening.

Varieties of early season tomatoes

There are a number of both hybrid and heirloom tomatoes with shorter transplant-to-harvest times and also may be slightly more tolerant to cooler spring temperatures. These early season tomatoes can be tasty but are often smaller than regular season tomatoes. Some of these varieties are described below.

Early Girl: This is the classic early-season producing tomato plant. It is not a particularly cold-resistant variety, but does have an extremely short 52 days from transplant to harvest. Early Girl is an indeterminate hybrid and does well in a variety of climates. It produces small, red fruit about the size of a tennis ball that is particularly good for salads. For a little tomato trivia, Early Girl was named as a partner to the already popular "Better Boy," which at the time was sold by the same seed company.

Whippersnapper: This is a cherry tomato variety that produces smooth, light-red oval fruits very early in the season. It is an indeterminate heirloom variety that has a small, compact bush habitat. Therefore, it is often recommended for hanging baskets or other containers. They are projected to produce in 52 days from transplanting.

Sub Arctic 25: This is an heirloom indeterminate variety developed in Canada for the local short season gardens. It is a standard variety found commonly in tomato gardens in interior Alaska, where average mid-summer temperatures hover around 60 degrees Fahrenheit, and the average length of the frost-free growing season is only around 120 days. Fruits tend to be 1 ½ to 2 inches in diameter and will set fruit even when nighttime temperatures are in the 40s.

Polar Baby: This is a determinate variety that was developed in Alaska and produces ripe fruit 60 days after transplanting. It is a reasonably sized fruit, about 2 inches in diameter, for an early season variety.

Oregon Spring: This is a cold-resistant variety developed by Oregon State University for short season gardeners. It is a determinate variety that grows on a small compact bush. It is almost normal size, good for slicing, and also good for producing a thick creamy juice.

Northern Exposure: This is a determinate hybrid variety that is bred for cooler, short-season areas. It produces generous-sized, deep red round fruit with 67 days from transplant to harvest.

Growing Mid- and Long-Season Tomatoes

Mid-season tomatoes are the most common tomato varieties, and generally will bear ripe fruit between 65 and 80 days after planting in the garden. Late-season tomatoes are generally the largest of the tomatoes and have a harvest date between 80 and 100 days after planting in the garden. Both hybrid and heirloom varieties of mid- and late-season tomatoes exist and are widely used. Late-season tomatoes will obviously be difficult to grow in northern sections of the country, but are very popular in other areas due to their size and taste.

There are a number of approaches specific to growing long-season tomatoes. Some of these approaches involve choosing specific varieties of tomato plants; others involve techniques for keeping plants healthy for the entire season and for managing through potentially cool weather in the early fall.

Tips and strategies for long-season tomatoes

Late in the season — as the weather begins to get cooler and wetter — one approach for offering protection to your late-producing plants is to selectively remove some of the green foliage. Removing some of the leaves allows more sunshine and wind to get to the plants and fruits and mitigate some of the effects of moisture and humidity. Also, it sometimes helps to pinch off new shoots or new flowers that develop in the two to three weeks before an anticipated frost. This helps focus the plant energy on fruit growth and ripening.

A major issue with trying to produce tomatoes late in the season is the prevalence of blight. Blight is a fungus-caused tomato disease that is often encouraged by the wet cooler days of the late summer and early fall. Fungicides are available that are effective against many versions of late blight, although to be effective, they must be applied as a preventative measure before the plants have been infected. Check your plants regularly for signs of infection. You can recognize blight from the dark spots or lesions on the leaves. There are several Web sites with photos of various kinds of diseases and blight to aid in identification. One example is the Texas A&M Extension Service Web site (**http://aggie-horticulture.tamu.edu/publications/tomatoproblemsolver**). Another great site for diagnosing garden maladies was created at Cornell University and is called Vegetable MD Online (**http://vegetablemdonline.ppath.cornell.edu**). If you find evidence of blight, it is important that you remove any diseased plants immediately, as the fungus will spread.

Popular varieties of long-season tomatoes

As with early tomatoes, there are a number of both hybrid and heirloom varieties that have a longer growing term than typical tomato plants. In general, the time from transplant to harvest for these varieties is around 80 days or greater. Long-season varieties tend to be the ones that produce the largest fruit. Following are some tomato varieties that are long-season producers:

Burpee Supersteak Hybrid: This is a large fruit variety that matures in 80 days and produces fruit that averages about 2 pounds in weight. It is an indeterminate variety great for slicing on sandwiches and burgers.

Big Mama Hybrid: These are large, plum-shaped sauce tomatoes that mature in 80 days. They are an indeterminate variety that is very meaty and particularly good for making sauces.

Believe it or Not: A large, red, smooth heirloom indeterminate variety. It is not unusual to get fruits of 2 pounds from this plant. They are good for slicing and for making tomato juice.

Popular varieties of mid-season tomatoes

Celebrity: This is one of the most popular varieties of tomatoes. It is a hybrid that is often recommended by county extension agents, as it is a good size, produces well, and is disease resistant. While it is classified as a determinate, it is a fairly large plant that is sometimes hard to distinguish from an indeterminate.

Big Boy: This is a classic hybrid variety of tomato that Burpee developed in 1949 that continues to be a popular tomato in home gardens, especially in the South. It is an indeterminate variety with a sprawling vine and can produce fruits up to one pound each.

Better Boy: This hybrid is literally the son of the Big Boy variety and was developed with more disease resistance than the father plant. This is a very popular cultivar and is a standard in many home gardens. It is indeterminate and grows into a sprawling plant that will need strong support and some pruning. *For more information on the Better Boy, see Chapter 2 — it was referenced as one of the popular types for slicing.*

Sweet 100: This is probably the most popular cherry tomato. It is an indeterminate hybrid that is very disease-resistant and will produce literally hundreds of tomatoes. Suckers (side shoots between the stem and a branch) grow abundantly on this variety and some pruning will be desirable and will not limit fruit production.

Juliet: This may be the most popular variety of grape tomatoes. It is an indeterminate hybrid variety with a very sweet flavor that has won several tasting contests. The seeds are widely available to home gardeners.

Lemon Boy: This is another Burpee hybrid that is unique as the fruit is a bright lemon-yellow color when it is ripe. It is a vigorously growing indeterminate variety that is resistant to a variety of diseases. It has a sweet but tangy, distinctive flavor.

Supporting Tomatoes

To support or not to support

While many gardeners do not attempt it, tomatoes can be grown without support and allowed to spread over the ground. Indeterminate varieties will essentially grow into vines that will lie comfortably on the ground. This requires significantly more space and runs more risk of damage to the fruit from pests or disease. A thick layer of compost is helpful to keep plants and particularly fruit from direct contact with the soil. Furthermore, some small or dwarf determinate varieties can actually stand unsupported in either the garden or in patio containers, although they will be at risk in windy or stormy weather.

A typical gardener will look to some type of support structure. Supporting your tomato plants will allow you to grow significantly more tomato plants in the same space. It will also likely increase your tomato production per plant. If wildlife pests are a problem for your garden site, supporting plants can also keep the fruit out of reach of some animals like rabbits and raccoons. Squirrels are adept climbers and can even reach fruit on supported plants, but accomplish this with much more difficulty than on unsupported plants. Also, unsupported plants tend to put fruit more at risk of attack by soil-based diseases or soil-based insects.

Staking

Staking was once the most common approach for managing tomato plants for both home and commercial gardens, but is now only used by home gardeners because it is somewhat labor intensive. If staking is the support of choice, it should be done very soon after transplanting to avoid damage to rapidly expanding root systems. The requirement for stake height will be different for different varieties of tomatoes, but a standard height is about 6 feet tall with roughly 10 to 12 inches of the stake underground. Decay-resistant wood is best and if used can be reused for multiple seasons. Cutting a point into the end of the stake makes it easy to drive into the ground for 12 inches. Ties will be used to tie the stem loosely to the stake at roughly every 12 inches. Soft twine can be used to tie the tomatoes, but strips of rags are more desirable, as they are less likely to cut into the tomato stem. When staking, some pruning is probably best to better manage the plant. Pruning can help keep a plant reasonably well controlled, so that two main vines develop close to the base of the plant. Staking tomatoes is pretty simple and not very costly, but it can be somewhat time and labor intensive as the tomato plants grow. It is necessary to tie and re-tie vines and branches on a weekly basis and to salvage the occasional toppled stake and plant that fall after a major storm.

Cages

Tomato cages are probably the most popular type of support for tomatoes among home gardeners. This is due to the wide availability of cages. You can find pre-formed cages of several sizes in discount stores, nurseries, and home improvement stores. They are also very easy to use and easy to install. Like stakes, they should be put in place soon after transplanting plants into the garden to avoid any disruption of the developing root system and to allow the plant to grow into the cage. Cages also allow tomatoes to grow with minimum pruning, as the cage tends to easily support growing branches and vines. Pre-formed cages made specifically for tomato and pepper plants can be purchased. These cages can be somewhat flimsy and will often need to be staked to assure they do not topple when the plants get larger. With proper care, cages will last several years before needing to be replaced. All metal cages will rust over time, but surface rust serves a protective function — it prevents further rust, and the cages will still function well for several years. The primary reason these cages do not last more than a few years is because they are somewhat flimsy and the wires will finally bend or break. The store-bought cages are constructed to be narrower at the bottom than the top. As a result, these store-bought cages can be stacked and stored more easily.

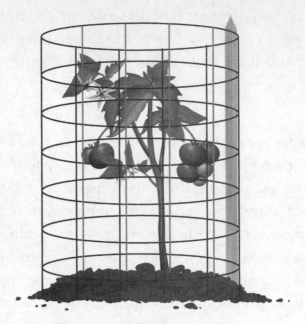

DIAGRAM 5: TOMATO WIRE CAGE

Another alternative for cages is to buy wire structures and create your own cages. Concrete reinforcing mesh or animal wire fencing are good options for homemade cages. Cages formed from these wires tend to be somewhat more durable and will generally survive more seasons. The hole size in the wire mesh is generally large enough to allow easy harvesting through the mesh. The wire structure is cut in roughly 5- to 6-foot sections and curved into a column-like structure and secured with twine or wire. These structures can be reinforced with stakes or anchored to the ground with U-shaped stakes. The downside of the cages that you make from wire fencing or reinforcing mesh is they tend to be more difficult to break down and if not broken down, can be cumbersome and space intensive to store over the winter. One strategy to more easily manage the homemade cages over the winter is to build cages that differ in size by a few inches, so they can be nested without deconstructing.

DIAGRAM 6: FLORIDA WEAVE TOMATO

Florida-weave post and twine support

The trellis system is another support system that is similar to ones used in much commercial tomato production. Using posts and twine, the trellis system is easy and economical to construct and tends to be one of the more space-efficient supports for tomato plants. Posts should be 2 inches wide, and nylon or natural fiber twine can be used, although nylon will tend to stretch less as the tomato plants grow heavier. In this system, a row of wooden stakes is set in the ground, with the stakes set 8 to 12 inches deep. There should be about 5 feet between each stake. Two tomato plants are planted between each set of stakes. Once the tomato plants have grown about 18 to 24 inches tall, install the first twine support at about 12 inches above the soil line. Tie twine to one end of the row and weave the twine down one side the tomato plants and around each stake, returning down the row on the other side of the plants so the twine is on both sides of each tomato plant. Continue adding more twine horizontal supports as the tomato plants grow. An alternative pattern can be used by weaving the nylon string or twine around each tomato plant, so the plants are also a little more supported from sliding between the strings. Pruning will be necessary for this support structure to keep tomato plants under control. Prune by pinching off suckers that grow below the flower clusters. Some gardeners also pinch off the tomato tops when they grow beyond the height of the stakes. When growing determinate cultivars using this weave method, only prune once to remove the first suckers or your tomato yield will suffer.

String trellis support

Another interesting approach, for managing and controlling vine growth is using strings hung from an overhead beam to support the growing tomato plants. This approach is more appropriate for indeterminate varieties that can be pruned to fit the trellis support system. Several approaches can be used for constructing the vertical posts and the horizontal top beam. One approach, described by the Master Gardeners of the Santa Clara County Extension Service, uses electrical conduits for both the vertical and horizontal supports. Other systems use wooden posts with a heavy wire run at the top of the posts for the horizontal support. Vertical supports are placed no more than 10 feet apart and the horizontal beam is placed roughly 6 feet from the ground. One end of a long piece of heavy natural fiber twine is tied loosely around the bottom of each tomato plant and then woven up around the tomato plant stems. The other end of the twine is tied to the horizontal beam. As the plant grows, the twine can be twisted more around each stem. With this method, plants within a row can be grown reasonably close together (18 to 24 inches) and extra room can be left between the rows for easy access and easy weeding. For this type of support, the plant should be pruned to limit growth to one or two main stems. If two stems are desired, a second string should be dropped to support the second stem. This approach can be very space efficient in the garden and the support pieces can be easily disassembled to store compactly in the garden shed or garage. The downside of this approach is that like staking, it can require regular monitoring as the plant grows to assure that the plant stem stays twisted around the string supports.

Smart Companion Plants With Tomatoes

Cooking companions

A primary objective in choosing companion plants for the tomato garden is strictly a culinary objective. There are some particular vegetables and herbs that blend well with tomatoes, are easy to grow, and ensure that you will get the most value and enjoyment out of your crop. The following is a short list of some popular culinary companion plants:

Basil: Basil is an extremely easy plant to grow in either the garden or in containers on the front porch. It is used fresh in salads and sauces with tomatoes and can be fairly pricey to buy fresh in the market.

Oregano: Also an easy herb to grow, but easier to manage in a container. Several varieties exist that have different flavor twists. Oregano is a staple in tomato sauces and in many styles of bruschetta.

Peppers: Peppers are of the same nightshade family as tomatoes and also turn up in various stews, sauces, and salads with tomatoes. They are very prolific and, for fresh use, require only a couple of plants. Peppers can also be found in tomato-based parmigianas or lasagnas.

Eggplant: The eggplant is also a relative of the tomato plant. Like the pepper, they also appear in a variety of Italian tomato-based dishes. They are popular with vegetarians and are commonly used as a meat replacement in lasagnas or grilled dishes. Another reason for growing eggplant is the availability of diverse and tasty varieties in the form of plants and seeds — more than the usual supermarket selection.

Growing companions

The second companion planting objective is the more conventional agricultural objective of choosing plants that will improve the growth of your tomato plants. Gardeners can accomplish this by growing companion plants in close proximity to the tomato plants. The objective of the companion plant is either to enhance the soil for the tomato plants or to reduce the threat of particular diseases or pests as a result of the proximity of the companion plant. Often, companion plants are chosen that will attract insect populations to act as predators to disease-causing organisms. In other situations, the companion plant actually produces natural insect repellents to discourage insects that attack the tomato plant.

Companion planting is one of those gardening subjects that is somewhat polarizing. It is very popular among some gardeners, but also has some avid detractors who regard it as folklore. As with many similar situations, the truth is probably somewhere in the middle of the two. While companion planting is surely not a panacea for pest and disease control, it does add some measure of protection or enrichment. Companion planting can also be a challenge due to the timing, space, and management issues. This is a great area to explore with your local extension service and to let your own personal experimentation guide you. The following are a few of the more common and accepted companion plants for tomatoes:

Borage: Borage is an annual plant that produces a cucumber-like vegetable and is also dried and used as an herb. It is one of the most popular companion plants for a variety of vegetables including tomatoes. In the case of tomatoes, it repels the tomato hornworm and is also cited for improving flavor and growth.

Marigolds: Marigolds are also a popular companion plant and is known to have a deterrent effect on nematodes, beetles, and some varieties of tomato worms. As they produce an attractive yellow or gold flower, they also are good for improving the garden curb appeal.

Basil: Basil is sometimes planted near tomato plants as a boost to flavor and growth. Basil is very aromatic and is often cited as a deterrent to flies and mosquitoes.

Cabbage: Tomatoes and garlic have been shown to be good companion plants for cabbage. Studies in Mexico over a three-year period found that when tomatoes were planted near cabbage, insect damage to the cabbage was reduced and yields were improved.

Asparagus: Tomato plants are also cited to be good at improving an asparagus crop when planted close by, as the tomato plant is a deterrent to the asparagus beetle.

And on the other end of the spectrum, avoid planting tomatoes in any proximity to black walnut trees. The leaves, roots, and bark of the black walnut contain a chemical that is toxic or growth-stunting to members of the nightshade family, including tomatoes.

A good resource for information on companion planting was created by the National Sustainable Agricultural Information Service and can be found on the web at **http://attra.ncat.org/attra-pub/complant.html**.

Chapter 6:
Tomato Care Through the Seasons

Watering

The fact that plants need water is intuitive and undebated, but few novice gardeners can tell you why plants need water. The plant uses water as part of photosynthesis, which is the process unique to plants allowing them to essentially make their own food; a key skill that humans and animals have never enjoyed. In this process, plants use sunlight to convert carbon dioxide from the air into sugars, which are used to feed plant and aid in fruit growth. Another function of water is to dissolve and carry nutrients in the soil into the roots and through the plant. The majority of water that enters the roots is actually lost from the plant through the leaves as the leaves transpire or "breathe" to absorb carbon dioxide. This water loss through the leaves drives the pressure to pull more water up from the roots and also contributes to evaporative cooling of the plant — essentially, it is how plants breathe and sweat. During dry periods when water to the plant is limited, the plant will close its leaf stoma or pores and shut down transpiration. This shutdown of the leaf pores will deprive the plant of carbon dioxide, limiting photosynthesis and overall growth.

Watering systems

Sprinklers are still the most common approach for watering home gardens, including tomato plants. Sprinklers have the advantage of being low cost, easy to set up, and easy to maintain. It is also easy to share your sprinkler system between your garden and your lawn or landscaping. However, watering tomatoes (and other parts of the garden) with sprinklers has some significant disadvantages.

Sprinklers deliver water directly to the leaves and stems of tomato plants while water is predominately absorbed only by the roots of plants. In greenhouses, plants can grow healthily without their leaves ever seeing any water. Furthermore, sprinklers tend to distribute water across the foliage, leaves, and other surfaces around the garden. This tends to waste a meaningful amount of water, sometimes when water use in communities is at its peak and over-consumption is discouraged. While most communities will limit bans on watering to lawns and landscaping and exempt vegetable gardens, it is still prudent from an economic and conservation perspective to be efficient in your water application. Mud is another undesirable by-product of watering with sprinklers. Mud not only makes for a messy experience when entering the garden, but also tends to compact the soil. Watering with sprinklers on the plants and in the rows between the plants also tends to encourage weed growth.

Applying water to your plants with sprinklers can encourage the spread of disease. A regularly damp and humid environment around tomato plant foliage tends to encourage the growth of fungi, molds, and bacteria that can contribute to various tomato plant diseases or blights. In addition, regularly splashing soil onto the tomato plants and foliage can spread soil onto the surface of the leaves. This allows for potential contamination with disease-causing organisms in the soil, which can lead to blight. Some dedicated gardeners will even cover their tomato plants with a sheet of clear polyethylene in the late part of the summer to avoid the late summer rains, which can contribute to tomato blight. Keep the covering from contacting the tomato plants and foliage. You can also cover the plants with it early in the season and leave the covering in place, as it will act as a pseudo-greenhouse and contribute some warmth in the spring.

Watering your tomatoes by hand with a hose generally does not work for more than one or two tomato plants. Water applied by hand is always applied far too quickly, and most of the water runs off rather than soaking deeply into the soil. For more than one or two plants, the amount of water needed would challenge even the most patient gardener. Drip or trickle application systems are much preferred for most vegetable gardens and particularly for tomato plants. In drip systems, water is applied directly to the base of the plants in a slow trickle through hoses or tubes. Drip systems allow water to be delivered directly to your plants slowly and efficiently. It has been estimated that water use can be reduced by 50 percent with drip watering systems for the garden. It also tends to minimize erosion that occurs when you inadvertently overwater with sprinklers.

Drip irrigation systems do require some financial investment upfront, but most of the system is reusable from year to year. It also requires some time investment initially to measure, calculate, and design the system for your garden. Depending on the layout and type of garden, parts of a drip irrigation system may need to be removed and stored every year to allow for tilling and soil recovery. Despite the investment in time and labor, the rewards of choosing a drip system over sprinkling are significant — and have been documented in multiple agricultural studies — in water savings and plant yield.

Soaker hoses are one of the types of drip irrigation that many gardeners use. Soaker hoses are rubber garden hoses with thousands of tiny holes along and around the hose. Water seeps out of the holes in the hose and provides a slow and steady source of water directly to your plants. Soaker hoses come in a variety of diameters with different spacing and sizes of the holes.

Drip or trickle tape is the other approach for drip irrigation. These systems are similar to systems used by professional growers. The principle is the same, but in this case water is provided through plastic tubing that is perforated with small holes at different intervals ranging from 8 to 24 inches. The spacing that you select is mostly dependent on the type of soil that you have, with sandier soils using a smaller spacing.

Both systems — soaker hoses or drip tape — require a pressure regulator to reduce the pressure coming out of your garden faucet from the typical home water pressure of 60 to 80 psi (pounds per square inch) to around 30 psi. In addition, you will need a filtration cartridge to reduce the likelihood of plugging up the soaker hose or drip tape. In both cases, one row of tape or hose is laid down for every row of tomato plants about 2 to 3 inches from the plants. The tape or hose can be put on top of the mulch, on top of the soil, or just beneath the soil. In general, between the soil and mulch is the simplest method and makes for easier maintenance. Some also choose to include a timer to ensure that those early-morning watering sessions are not forgotten.

Soaker hoses are used for home gardens, but are limited to about 200 feet in length for a bed. They also tend to plug more frequently than drip tapes, so may require flushing or maintenance more often.

Timing

How often you should water your tomato plants depends on various factors including your local climate, the amount of rainfall, the type of soil in your garden, and if you use mulch. During extremely dry periods, a good rule of thumb is to thoroughly water your plants every two to three days. When relying on rainfall, the minimum requirement for tomato plants is roughly 1 inch of water per week and up to 1 ½ inches in the heat of the summer. In dry periods, container plants can need watering on a daily basis to keep them healthy and strong. When plants are watered, they should be watered thoroughly to saturate at least 8 to 10 inches of soil. This is particularly important early in the season, as shallow root systems are first developing. More frequent watering will encourage the development of a shallow root system. Water frequently enough to prevent severe wilting of the plants. Some recoverable wilting of plants will happen on particularly hot summer days and is not necessarily a sign of a need for water.

Over-watering can be almost as damaging to your tomato plants as under-watering. Too much water too fast will cause runoff, erosion, and loss of nutrients from the garden soil.

The type of soil that you have may not necessarily impact how much water your tomato plants require but will affect watering requirements. More sandy soils will drain more quickly, so water the plants in lesser amounts but more often.

Particularly in the early part of the season, tomato plants should be watered early in the day. Watering in the morning will allow the sun to warm the soil during the day and keep the average temperature of the soil higher. Early morning watering is especially important when using sprinklers, as this will give the plant foliage more opportunity to dry during the day and reduce the leaf moisture that can encourage disease. Throughout the season, watering during cooler and cloudy days or parts of the day will minimize evaporative losses and cost.

Dry gardening

Every location does not have the benefit of an abundant and regular supply of water. Home gardeners have adopted some techniques from commercial growers that are used in arid climates with limited water to grow a variety of vegetables, including tomatoes. These techniques are typically called dry farming, and are common in parts of California and the Southwest. Of course, the approach does not mean "no-water gardening," but does try to grow with a minimum amount of added water. There is also some evidence that better fruit is produced under drier conditions. A recent study by the University of California Santa Cruz Agroecology Department found that tomatoes grown under dry gardening conditions were more flavorful than tomatoes grown with drip irrigation. The idea here is that the reduced moisture in the plant — and consequently in the fruit — concentrates the flavor. The basic approach for growing tomatoes under dry gardening conditions is the following:

1. **Amend your soil to collect and retain as much water as possible.** Add generous amounts of aged compost or manure to the garden. A good target is to add ½ inch of compost or manure in the fall and in the spring. Organic matter improves the soil in general but also helps build the soil so that it will retain more water. Soils should be worked down to about 12 inches to maximize the potential water-holding capacity of the soil. In particular, sandy soils have poor water-holding capability, so you will need to aggressively compost to be able to make these soils hold water. Once your tomatoes are planted, mulching is critical to limit evaporation of moisture from the soil. A number of different types of mulches will serve the purpose, so use whatever is available in your area. A combination of newspaper and leaves, grass clippings, or straw works well to create this mulch. The mulch will protect the soil from drying winds and scalding sun. It will also serve the purpose of preventing the growth of weeds that steal water from the soil.

2. **Choose the right plants and give them space.** There are a few tomato varieties that are more resistant to dry conditions than others, so focus on choosing these cultivars. Some of these include the Porter tomato, an heirloom indeterminate that matures in 65 to 80 days; the Sunmaster tomato, a determinate hybrid that tolerates both heat and dry conditions better than typical varieties; and the Great White Beefsteak Tomato, which is an indeterminate variety that produces large white fruit that is heat and drought tolerant. If your dry weather is especially focused in the mid to late summer, focus on short season tomato varieties that will mature before the driest weather arrives.

The Early Girl short season tomato is very popular for dry farming among commercial growers in California. Before garden planting, allow transplants to develop in at least 4-inch pots to encourage root growth before transplanting. Water thoroughly during this phase. When transplanting, remove several of the lowest leaves and plant deeply to encourage more root growth. For dry gardening, plants should be planted further apart than is typically specified. Spacing them as far apart as four to five feet is desirable if the space is available. This will allow roots to spread liberally and build a strong support system for the upcoming dry months. To survive a dry season, tomato plants need to have developed a strong, extensive root system.

3. **Water young transplants early and then let them manage on their own.** Watering thoroughly and allowing soil to dry out between watering is important for young transplants. In many climates, this allows you to take advantage of the more frequent spring rains and tolerate the dry summer months. When the transplants are well established, you can cut back on watering. Once plants set fruit, they should be able to survive without additional watering beyond rainfall. While the plants may wilt somewhat in the afternoon sun, if the root systems are strong, they can survive dry periods better than you might expect.

CASE STUDY: TIMELESS TOMATO TIPS

Harry McCorkle
Long-time home gardener
Bonaire, Georgia

Harry McCorkle was born in 1925 and has been growing tomatoes and other vegetables for more than 50 years. Like many home gardeners, McCorkle has grown vegetables partly as a food source and partly as a hobby. He shares some of his tips for growing tomatoes here.

Home tomato gardening is a pursuit that spans multiple generations. McCorkle always was generous to friends, family, and neighbors with his consistent surplus of crops. And still, every year by the end of the garden season, he and his wife, Claudine, always had a freezer over-filled with tomatoes, peas, butter beans, and corn; and a pantry stacked high with jars of canned tomatoes, beans, and pickles. "At one point, I grew 80 tomato plants," McCorkle said, "but as I got into my eighties, I slowed down and now only put in 15 to 20 plants."

One of the more interesting strategies that McCorkle uses is "planting" an empty gallon-sized pot 6 inches from each of his tomato plants. He typically uses the gallon-sized plastic pots that plants often come in from the nursery. He cuts the bottom out of the pot, drills three holes each about 1 inch in diameter around the side of the pot, and buries it so the top is just about even with the soil line. He adds the water and fertilizer that he uses for his plants to the pot. This allows him to target the soil and root systems and avoids soil erosion or the washing away of valuable fertilizer. McCorkle said, "I add a handful of 10-10-10 fertilizer to each pot every ten days. This allows me to better control my water and fertilizer addition. I lime the ground six months before planting time. I also like to put a handful of peanut meal underneath each transplant as I plant them but avoid having the meal make direct contact with the roots." McCorkle uses three to four layers of newspaper covered with composted leaves as mulch for his garden. He is a fan of hybrid tomatoes and tries to choose those varieties that have the highest disease resistance.

"I learned pretty much everything I know about planting tomatoes from an old-timer who had been planting tomatoes for 40 years when I met him," McCorkle said. "While you can buy more different tomato varieties now than you used to be able to, other things about tomato growing just don't change."

Mulching

Mulching is one of those activities that calls for an investment in time and labor up front that pays back later in the season. There is good experimental support for the benefit of mulches. Mulch — if chosen and used properly — can both increase the total yield of your tomato crop and can hasten the production and ripening of early season tomatoes. Mulches — both synthetic and organic — can contribute to reducing the spread of disease by preventing the splashing of soil up onto the tomato plant and fruit. As pointed out in the discussion on watering, they can contribute to a more efficient use of water and fertilizer — and consequently, money. The following is a list of some of the materials that have been popularized as mulches in the tomato garden. There is certainly no requirement to use only one type of mulch, so mix them depending on availability and cost.

Black plastic: This is the classic synthetic mulch and is made from black, low-density polyethylene (LDPE) film. Black plastic has become the standard mulch for commercial growers based on both its ease of use and the data supporting its benefits. Agricultural data shows that 30 million acres of commercial agricultural land worldwide was covered in black plastic in 1999. Plastic film provides a complete barrier to weeds and is reasonably easy to apply to the garden. Unlike some organic mulch, black plastic has the advantage of not carrying the likelihood of bringing along other undesirable components, such as pesticides, weed seeds, insects, or disease-causing organisms. Plastic film mulch is traditionally black, as the dark color causes the absorption of more heat from the sun and warms the soil more quickly in the spring. Because of this warming effect, in southern climates the black plastic should be covered with organic mulch as the summer heat increases, to prevent the soil from getting too hot. The major disadvantage of plastic film is the labor and expense involved in removing the film every year. Even organic gardeners have recognized the benefit of black plastic, and this has driven the development of bio-degradable black plastic film that has shown promise in experimental trials. Clear plastic has can also be used as a mulch, and while it will warm the soil even more effectively than the black plastic film, it will also create a greenhouse effect and encourage weeds to flourish.

Red plastic mulch: Red plastic film for mulch was introduced in the last decade based on some research that demonstrated increased productivity and yield for tomato plants when using this red film. The theory is that the red film reflects red light back onto the tomato plants and encourages more foliage growth. Other experiments find a reduction in soil nematodes when using red mulch. While other experiments have not documented an increase in tomato productivity and yield, most of the large seed and garden vendors now sell a version of the red plastic mulch.

Shredded rubber tires: Rubber-based mulch materials have appeared in the mulch departments of several of the large home improvement stores. The world produces far more used tires than the recycle market can absorb, so some of these tires end up as creative mulch materials. While these materials are long lasting and could be appropriate for some mulching needs like paths or playgrounds, there is no good evidence that would support their use in the vegetable garden. They are hard to remove from the garden after the season and do not readily degrade; therefore, making for poor soil amendments.

Hay/straw: Both hay and straw can be used effectively as organic mulch. They are typically available in most nurseries and also in feed stores. Apply either of these materials liberally, as both decompose reasonably quickly and will need to be reinforced as the season progresses. Like other organic mulches, the decomposition has the benefit of naturally amending the soil. Both hay and straw provide good weed control. Hay or straw should not be applied to the ground early in the season, as they tend to insulate the soil and keep the soil temperature cooler.

Grass clippings: Grass clippings are often readily available from your own yard or from your neighbors and can make very economical mulch. U.S. Department of Agriculture (USDA) research indicates that decomposing grass clippings contribute to reducing the population of nematodes in the soil and increasing tomato yield. This is apparently related to the ammonia produced as the grass clippings decompose. As with all organic mulches, clippings should be used generously, applying at least 2 inches to effectively manage weed control. Grass clippings can be used directly from the lawn or can be composted for a short period. Clippings from grass that has been treated in the last few days with pesticides or herbicides should be used with caution.

Leaves: Leaves are another often readily available mulching material that might be collected from your yard or from the neighbors. Leaves are best if shredded or allowed to partially decompose before use, making them less likely to blow around the garden. Leaves should be applied to a depth of 2 to 3 inches. Like other organic materials, leaves are a desirable type of mulch, as they can be easily tilled into the soil at the end of the season to provide organic matter for the soil.

Sawdust: Sawdust can provide good mulch for a tomato garden; a 2- to 3-inch layer will provide excellent weed control. Sawdust is generally available from sawmills or wood shops and is pretty economical. In contrast to some other organic materials, sawdust contains mostly carbon and very little nitrogen. As a result, it will tend to need nitrogen to decompose and can end up competing with your tomato plants for nitrogen. If you choose to use sawdust as mulch, add high-nitrogen fertilizer to the sawdust to compensate and to facilitate the sawdust decomposition.

Bark/wood Chips: Several inches of bark or shredded wood chips will make effective mulch for weed and moisture control. Shredded wood chips are preferred in the tomato garden, as they will decompose more readily than bark. Like sawdust, adding a high-nitrogen fertilizer is helpful for promoting more rapid decomposition.

Newspapers: Three to four layers of newspaper make very effective mulch. Newspaper is readily available and cheap, and will usually decompose after a growing season. Often, gardeners will use newspaper as the bottom mulch layer and add an inch or so of an organic type of mulch on top of the newspaper to hold it in place.

Weeding

Ideally, if you are diligent about applying and keeping the garden around your tomato plants mulched effectively, weeds will not be much of a problem. When growing tomato varieties without pruning, the tomato plants will produce a good deal of foliage that will shade the garden and keep weeds down to a minimum. If these strategies do not manage the weeds in your garden, do not ignore them. Weeds will compete with tomatoes for nutrients, water, and sunlight. If they are allowed to grow too aggressively, they can provide harbor for insect pests or diseases that can be threats to your tomatoes. While commercial growers will resort to herbicide for some weed control, this is an extreme measure for the home gardener. If you choose not to use mulch, allowing space between rows for tilling — as well as pulling or trimming weeds — is important for control. Loose soil that is generated by tilling the paths between the tomato plants can be raked around the base of the tomato stems to cover germinating weed seeds and provide a bit of "dust mulch" around the plants.

Another factor to consider is the growth of grasses and weeds in close proximity to the garden. Tall weeds and grasses close to the garden provide a perfect home for rabbits, moles, or other small pests that might find snacks in your garden appealing. It definitely pays to have the perimeter of your garden free from overgrowth.

Pruning

The idea behind pruning tomato plants is pretty straightforward. First, limiting the growth of foliage will force the plant to focus on fruit development and maturation. Second, removing some of the plant foliage will provide better access to air and light for the remaining foliage and will reduce the likelihood of disease. There are two primary factors that determine when and how you choose to prune your tomato plants: the type of tomato plant and the type of support you have chosen for your plant. Before any more detail on pruning, the following is a brief primer on how tomato plants grow.

The basics of tomato plant growth

As described previously in the book, tomato plants fall into two primary categories that describe the growth habit of the plant — determinate and indeterminate.

Determinate varieties will grow only to a pre-determined height based on the particular variety. They are shorter, bushier, and more compact than indeterminate varieties. New branches form from the inside of the elbow formed between older branches and the main stem. These side shoots are often called suckers. Flower clusters are formed after every two sets of leaves.

Indeterminate varieties will continue to grow almost indefinitely in height, limited only by what support is provided for them. With indeterminates, flower clusters are generally produced after every third leaf structure. Indeterminates will also produce suckers, which, if allowed, will grow indefinitely. This would create plants with multiple highly branched stems. Suckers that form closer to the ground will grow the most vigorously as a result of their proximity to the roots and increased levels of sugar found lower in the plant. As the plant gets taller and taller, sucker production and the robustness of sucker growth will diminish.

Pruning strategies

The best pruning is done by regularly managing the suckers that are produced. Gardeners can easily pinch off suckers with their fingers when the plants are young. Pinching off the sucker with your fingers when it is small and tender is called simple pruning. If the suckers are ignored and allowed to grow into stems, they may become too tough for finger pinching. In this case, snip them with sharp scissors or shears at a point just beyond the first leaves, rather than close in next to the stem. This will help prevent damage to the stem. This is sometimes referred to as 'Missouri pruning.' In some areas, all suckers are pruned this way to provide the plant with a little more foliage; therefore, providing shade protection from sunscald. Because determinate tomato growth is self-limiting, many gardeners choose not to prune them at all. Some recommend removing suckers below the level of the first flower cluster, but never remove suckers above the first flower cluster. For determinates, pruning above the first flower cluster will reduce the production of future fruit.

For indeterminate varieties, pruning is done to constrain the plant to a limited number of stems. In many cases, growers prefer one primary stem and will prune aggressively to maintain this stem. When using stakes or a trellis-type support system, pruning to maintain one or a maximum of two main stems is especially important. When using cages to support your plants, you can take the approach of forgoing all pruning. Well-constructed and tall cages can manage the most vigorous of indeterminate plants. Most gardeners will prune to try and control a maximum of three to four primary stems. Experiments in the field show that if you do not prune, it may not limit the overall production of an individual tomato plant; however, the average individual fruit size will become larger if pruned.

Another pruning strategy is used late in the season to encourage the plant to ripen existing fruit. It is a good idea to prune the top off of any remaining determinate plants and all indeterminate plants about three to four weeks before the first expected fall frost date. This will prevent the plant from wasting energy on more foliage production and encourage ripening of the green fruit that is on the plant, and limit the number of green tomatoes that you have to frantically pick before that first freezing night.

Fertilizing

The primary fertilizing for tomato plants is done as a part of the soil preparation process during the previous fall and in the early spring, before transplants are added into the garden. In addition, fertilizer and organic matter should be added when the transplants are first planted in the garden. Still, regular side dressings (adding about 1 to 2 tablespoons of additional fertilizer) are a good idea. Side dressings can be sprinkled on the soil next to each plant and worked into the surface of the soil. Fertilizers have a standard label designation that denotes the percentage of nutrients that they contain. The label will contain three numbers separated by dashed that refer to the percentage of nitrogen, phosphorous and potassium in that order, sometimes denoted as N-P-K. So, a bag of fertilizer that is labeled 10-5-10 contains 10 percent nitrogen, 5 percent phosphorous, and 10 percent potassium. The remaining 75 percent of material is filler or minor nutrients. The first addition of fertilizer to the soil is usually done when the first fruits are about 1 inch in diameter and scattered around the plant about 6 inches from the stem. After this point, further side dressings should be added every one to three weeks. If your soil tends to be sandy, you should add fertilizer more regularly because nutrients tend to be drained from the soil more rapidly. For soils that contain more clay, you can side dress less frequently. Working the fertilizer lightly into the soil is a good idea to keep it from being washed away. A slow watering is also good to more deeply drive the fertilizer into the soil if rain is not likely.

Chapter 7:
Non-Traditional Tomato Growing

For many reasons, not everyone will get the best results using traditional gardening techniques. With the diversity of climates, soils, available space, and the diversity of opinions among gardeners about time to invest and results expected, there are a number of new interesting approaches for growing tomatoes that have appeared over the years. This section will cover some of the most common and the most interesting variations on tomato gardens. This is an area where home gardeners have a huge advantage over commercial growers, as they have the flexibility to experiment with approaches that might only be possible on small scales.

Raised Beds

Using a raised bed is a popular gardening approach for a variety of vegetable and landscaping plantings. Raised beds are simply planting areas where the surface of the soil in the planted rows is roughly 8 to nine 9 inches higher than the path level between the rows. One way to think of it is that the to — and generally best part of the garden soil — is taken out of the paths between the rows where it would have been wasted and added to the planting rows where it can be advantageous. This gardening strategy became popularized in the early 1970s for some vegetable plants — particularly root plants like carrots and potatoes — that could benefit from the extra depth of good porous topsoil. It also became popular for landscaping shrubs and flowers and was used as a containment strategy.

Advantages

Raised beds offer several meaningful advantages to the home tomato gardener. They can be fairly labor intensive when you are first constructing them, but can be built to last many seasons. Keep in mind that raised beds are not for everyone.

Good soil depth: As tomatoes can have a very deep root system, a more generous depth of porous, aerated, and good draining topsoil will encourage root growth more deeply. This additional root depth will provide more access to soil moisture and nutrients and will provide more stability in windy or stormy weather.

Warmer soil: Constructing raised beds early in the spring will allow the top 8 to 9 inches of top soil to warm more effectively, which will encourage new tomato transplants that will grow both root structure and foliage more rapidly. As the season progresses in warmer climates, the raised beds must be mulched generously to prevent overheating of the soil around the tomato plants.

Soil improvement: If your soil is weak, construction of raised beds will allow you to concentrate your amendment and improvement efforts to the soil in the planting area and ignore the walking paths between your beds. This can be a cost savings in the purchase of soil amendments.

Drainage: Gardening in raised beds will also allow for better soil drainage in the planted rows, which can sometimes be a difficult problem during spring rains. In periods of heavy rain, water will drain into the paths between the raised beds leaving the raised areas to dry more quickly. This may make garden access a muddy business, but it does keep the roots of the tomato plants aerated.

Aesthetics: If your tomato garden is located in a visible and accessible area of your yard, constructing a raised bed can improve the curb appeal of your garden and make it 'front yard' presentable. By the choice of appropriate building materials, the raised beds can become a feature in your yard where a normal tomato garden may have looked inappropriate.

Construction options

The simplest raised beds are basically temporarily raised rows with no side supports made only to last for one growing season. The row widths should be between 2 and 4 feet, and the footpaths between the beds should be 2 to 3 feet to give ample access room to the beds. Beds should be raised in the early spring to allow plenty of time for the raised soil to warm. The area for the raised bed rows should be outlined with string first. Topsoil in the walking paths is simply raked or shoveled into the raised beds and raked flat. If you have a lot of garden area planned, you can also use a power garden tiller with a furrow attachment to run down the walking paths and push soil into the planting rows on either side.

Build a more substantial and permanent raised bed with wood planks for the sides and ends. You can recover wood from old decking or fencing wood. Treated wood is best used for this purpose, as the wood will be in contact with wet soil and will eventually rot if not treated. There is a potential concern with the treatment chemistry leaching out of the wood, but Environmental Protection Agency (EPA) studies have confirmed that contaminate levels from aging treated wood are exceptionally low. Wood for the sides should be at least 1 inch wide and even thicker if the beds are longer than 6 feet. Cinder block, brick, or stone can also be used to construct a more permanent raised bed. Numerous gardening supply stores and Web sites will also offer preformed materials designed for constructing raised beds of wood, plastic or stone. Many seed supply companies also sell components for constructing raised beds. You can also find a variety of complete kits for putting together raised beds including siding and connectors at the big-box home improvement stores and Web sites. Some have specially designed corner pieces to add an aesthetic touch and to help prevent intruders from stumbling into your beds. Any type of watering that is used in a standard garden can be used in a raised bed garden, but a drip irrigation system will leverage the benefits of the better draining beds even more effectively. *For places to buy seeds and other gardening supplies, see Appendix A.*

CASE STUDY: TERRACED TOMATO GROWING

Jerry Sheppard
Square Foot/Terrace Gardener
Roswell, Georgia

Jerry Sheppard shares his experiences in growing tomatoes in his terraced garden.

Sheppard has a beautiful home north of Atlanta, Georgia and was set on a vegetable garden in his backyard. While he is lucky to have a large, scenic, sunny backyard, it is on a steep slope — making it difficult for gardening. As a retired engineer, he had some skills that came in handy in redesigning and rebuilding his backyard. "The fact is that I had no level place to put a garden," Sheppard said. "So I began building terraced areas behind railroad cross-tie walls. During the first year, I built a 28- by 6-foot area that was about 3 to 4 feet at the deepest point and 1 foot deep at the shallowest point. I filled all but the top foot with a combination of compost and original dirt. I loaded the entire top foot with a mix designed by the University of Georgia and the extension service. Knowing that tomatoes can grow very deep roots, I planted them to the back of the garden, so they had 1 foot of super dirt and 3 or 4 additional feet of reasonably good dirt. I planted one plant per square foot block and fertilized with Osmocote. I planted six Better Boys and two grape tomatoes. They produced so well that I cooked down and froze several gallons for sauces and soups — superb."

In classic engineering fashion, Sheppard was happy, but not satisfied with his first year's terrace garden. He continued to expand and improve. During the second year, he installed a drip-irrigation system and doubled the garden by going down the hill and building a 50- by 4-foot terraced garden. Since the dirt he bought the first year was so expensive, Sheppard decided to make his own mix the next year. He bought mushroom humus and garden mix, and mixed them about half and half for the top foot of soil.

Another improvement he made was to add permanent walking boards to maintain access without stepping in the soil. He planted Red Lightning and Burgundy Boy tomatoes. Says Sheppard, "The Lightnings remained small and did not have the taste that I prefer although they were beautiful. The Burgundys tasted great but became misshapen."

Even terraced gardens close to the house do not deter hungry invaders. When the deer showed up, Sheppard responded. He added a three-strand electric fence, but lightning hit it twice — then deer overran it dozens of times. Next year, he wants to re-build the fence and expand the garden. He has scent cups that he hopes will convince those veggie predators not to cross the fence next year.

Knowing your local environment is an important theme here. This concept applies not only to managing the steep slope, but also to the very local climate. Sheppard lives in a valley, and the temperature is cooler than in the surrounding area, sometimes by 8 degrees Fahrenheit.

Space-Intensive Tomato Growing

With more people than ever interested in local, healthy produce and intent on stretching the family income, the popularity of home gardening continues to grow. Also, while the size of the average new home in the United States has been growing, the size of the average yard is getting smaller. With this, more gardeners are embarking on home growing with limited available garden-worthy space. Where space is limited, you can stretch your options with space-intensive gardening techniques. Tomatoes are one of the many vegetables where you can use some of these strategies to get the most from your garden space. While tomatoes are already one of the most productive vegetables in the garden, space-intensive techniques can push yields up to 60 pounds of tomatoes per 10-foot row.

Strategies

Support: The type of support that you choose contributes much to the tomato yield per square foot that you are able to produce. As a general rule, both staking and a Florida weave post and twine system are very space efficient. Use stakes if you only want to plant three to five tomato plants. Use the Florida weave post and twine system if you plant more than five plants. With both approaches in intensive gardening, pruning down to one main stem is best for most indeterminate varieties. If you are set on using cages, a good approach is to use the concrete reinforcing wire to construct a 4 ½ foot diameter circle and plant three transplants within each cage with each plant about 6 to 8 inches from the cage. This will put the plant spacing at about 3 feet apart. The transplants will serve to lean on each other and you will get more mileage out of a minimum number of cages. This approach works better for determinate, bushier varieties.

Double rows: As with many vegetables, an easy strategy for maximizing your available space is to place two plants per row. This can be done easily with staked tomatoes by putting the tomatoes in a zigzag pattern within the row. Because of the taller, more vine-like growth, the indeterminate varieties do very well in this type of configuration. With careful staking and pruning, they can be placed as close as one foot apart. Determinate varieties with a shorter, bushier habit can be placed at spacings of 30 inches between plants. Other smaller vegetables can be planted three or four plants wide per row, but the center tomatoes will suffer in more than double rows. Planting more than two tomato plants per row will also make the center plants difficult to access, harvest, and maintain.

Sunny Spot: As you push to put tomato plants closer together, it becomes even more important to assure that you choose a spot in your garden that gets at least six to seven hours of direct sunlight per day. The extra shading that the dense foliage causes can limit growth when planted in areas where sunlight is limited.

Raised beds: For small gardens, the double-row concept will essentially mean that your garden will evolve into squares of about 4- by 4-foot, rather than rows. These squares can be in raised-bed form or in the conventional flat-garden layout. The benefits of raised beds — draining, soil improvement, and soil warming — all play out equally well in the space-intensive format.

Challenges and Opportunities

While good tomato yields can be accomplished while growing in a limited amount of space, there are a couple of challenges that you should be aware of. Space-intensive gardening is not the approach to use if the objective is to grow very large tomato fruit. You may get an equivalent number of tomatoes or sometimes even more tomatoes, but the average size of the fruit will be smaller than when you give your plants a lot of growing room. Also, in the space-intensive garden, focus extra attention on watching for signs of disease or distress. The close quarters can sometimes create more humidity, less air circulation, and less sunlight on the foliage, which can contribute to the development of some fungus-based diseases. This is another reason for ensuring that the space-intensive garden gets plenty of sunshine. Also, the close proximity of the tomato plants to their neighbors may make detecting signs of disease or stress more difficult, so inspect regularly and closely.

Paths tend to be narrower with more turns when you lay out a tomato garden to maximize space. This may preclude the use of a power tiller to turn the soil and weed during the season. Weeding will need to be done by hand with hand tools. However, weeding tends to be less of a problem in space-intensive gardening, as your abundance of plants will crowd out competing weeds. Also, as the tomatoes are planted more compactly, it is easier to be more efficient with the use of both fertilizer and water.

Container Growing

Why grow in containers

Growing tomatoes is not just limited to the rural farmhouse or the suburban home with a yard. Tomatoes are one of the vegetables that adapt well to growing in containers on porches, front stoops, sun decks, or tenth-floor balconies. The only limitations in container possibilities are your minimum-size requirements and your imagination. The only requirement is a sunny spot, and even here you have some flexibility. Clever gardeners even place the tomato containers on wheels, so they can be moved from one side of the porch to the other every day and maximize their exposure to direct sunlight. Type the keywords "tomato" and "container" in to a search engine, and you will find scores of different container types that have been designed for tomato growing and are on sale through the Internet.

Container growing also has some advantages on both ends of the typical growing season. Plants can be planted in containers and moved outside early in the season as soon as the days warm up and moved inside only when nighttime temperatures are threatening. In the spring, soil in the containers will warm more quickly than garden soil and as a result, it is not unusual to get your first tomatoes from your container plants. At the end of the season, plants in containers can be moved inside to a basement or garage for the first frosty nights and then moved back outside as the summer moves through.

Finally, container plants can be less exposed to typical garden pests and diseases. Pests that live over the winter in your soil can be removed by sterilizing the soil with heat or hot water or by discarding the soil and starting over with new material. In containers on your deck, tomato plants are much less likely to be snacked on by hungry squirrels or deer.

Container size and type

The size of the container required for tomatoes will depend somewhat on the size of the variety that you have chosen. As a general rule, the depth of the pot should be at least 12 inches deep and at least 12 inches in diameter. Five-gallon containers are generally desirable for most varieties. Plastic pots, and in particular black plastic pots, will warm the soil more quickly than clay pots and will prevent soil from drying out as quickly as clay pots will allow. Be creative when choosing containers. Consider all kinds of options including construction buckets, old trash cans, bushel baskets lined with a garbage bag, or ceramic pots. Attractive and functional wood boxes can also be constructed so that your tomato garden becomes decorative as well as productive. As tomatoes are not fond of wet feet, any container should have drainage holes in the bottom to compensate for potential over-watering. Except for the smallest bush varieties, container plants will benefit from being staked or caged in a similar fashion to tomato plants in the garden.

Soil for containers

The safest planting medium for container gardening is to mix your own combination of peat moss, perlite, vermiculite, and compost. The soil mix should have enough stability and structure to support the root structure and plant, but also be porous enough to drain well. Garden soil can also be added to the mix, although this carries the risk of soil-borne disease or pests. A balanced 10-10-10 garden fertilizer should also be added per package directions.

Water and fertilizer for containers

Watering is probably the biggest challenge facing the tomato container gardener. Container tomato plants will need watering and fertilizing more often than tomato plants in the garden. They do not have the benefit of a large reservoir of garden soil around them from which to draw, and the root systems will be more limited than those of tomatoes in the garden. It is not unusual to need to water container tomatoes daily in the dry season. As with garden plants, apply water to the base of the stem and avoid wetting the plant foliage to limit the conditions for disease growth.

The best option for container tomatoes is to feed and water in one step daily. Make a fertilizer base solution to use for feeding the plants by mixing 2 cups of a standard fertilizer (say 10-20-10) in 1 gallon of warm water. Use 2 tablespoons of this base solution in 1 gallon of water as your daily water/feed solution. Once a week, give the plant a rest and flush the soil with a good dose of water alone.

Mulch for containers

As container-grown tomatoes tend to dry out even more quickly than plants in the garden, a good layer of mulch can be a plant-saver in dry spells. The same types of materials can be used although organic mulches are probably more appropriate than black plastic to allow access to rain water and to prevent splash-back onto plant foliage. Just as in the garden, a 2-inch layer of mulch will prevent weed growth and will prevent the soil from drying out as quickly.

Best tomato varieties for containers

Patio Princess: This is a dwarf hybrid variety bred specifically for size and compactness. Plants grow to about 2 feet in height and produce small fruit — about 2 to 3 inches. As this plant grows very small, you can place two to three plants in a large container.

Tomato Tumbler: This is a small hybrid variety of cherry tomatoes. It is determinate, but has long enough vines that it can adapt well to a hanging container. Fruit ripens very early — generally in 50 days from transplanting.

Bushsteak: This is a determinate variety that produces reasonably large fruit for a small plant. It only grows a couple of feet tall, but because of the weight of the fruit, it will require staking or some other kind of support.

Small Fry: This is a hybrid variety that produces a strong yield of small, bright red, cherry tomatoes on a medium-sized plant.

Growing Tomatoes Inside

If a year-round crop is what you are after and you do not have your own greenhouse, growing tomatoes inside is a reasonable — but not necessarily easy — option. There are a number of challenges to growing indoors but also several advantages. In particular, the control over growing conditions means little to no concern with pests and disease with your inside tomato plants.

Choose a determinate variety that produces a small stocky bush-type plant. A good option is cherry or grape tomatoes or some variety that produces a smaller fruit. Transplant your seedling into a 4- to 5-gallon container using a mix of potting soil, perlite, and peat moss as your planting medium. Garden soil is cheap but also tends to compact more readily and can harbor organisms or insects. Occasionally, you will need access to a sunny window to place your plant, but most often you will create your own light with a fluorescent light fixture. Even if you have a sunny window, proximity to a cold window can have a limiting effect on fruit set. When using a fluorescent light, set your light fixture on a timer and set it for 14 to 16 hours per day.

Inside plants will need to be watered and fertilized regularly. Daily or every-other-day watering is typical for the indoor, container-grown tomato. Dissolving fertilizer as described in the container gardening section is also good for using on indoor plants.

Unlike outside container-grown tomatoes, pollination may not necessarily come naturally if the plants are not exposed to any breeze or movement and you are not willing to harbor a few pollinating bees. Brushing the flower stems lightly with your hand or a cosmetic brush should provide enough vibration to encourage the pollen out of the male stamen and onto the female carpels. The time to conduct this pollination assist is when the flowers are fully opened and the yellow petals are turned back. Brush the stems for a few days during the middle of the day. Other techniques have been suggested, such as using the vibration of battery-powered toothbrushes or power razors to shake the flowers, but no data exists to demonstrate that these approaches are required. If the flower was successfully pollinated, the flower will wilt in a few days and the small ovary in the center of the flower will start to swell.

The other key requirement for a successful fruit set is the appropriate temperature for pollination and fruit set. The optimum temperature range for fruit set is between 65 and 80 degrees Fahrenheit. At temperatures below this range pollination and fruit set will be incomplete. At temperatures below 55 degrees Fahrenheit, fruit may set, but will often be misshapen. For this reason, growing tomatoes inside in a garage, basement, or other room that stays cool in the winter will likely not allow fruit to set effectively.

Unusual Growing Strategies

Upside-down tomatoes

There is a number of Internet sites and even a few television commercials extolling the virtues of the upside-down tomato. There are a number of specialty containers that are sold specifically for this purpose. However, the basic concept is essentially a container with a hole in the bottom where the tomato plant is placed. The proponents of this approach contend that the advantages offered include not having to stake or support the plant, space savings, and better flow of nutrients from the soil down the stem into the foliage. While botanists do not generally support the nutrient flow claim, there certainly is some benefit from space and the removal of the necessity for support. Watering the plant can be somewhat problematic as it will often flow out of the bucket and trickle down the stem of the plant. Also, root growth will not tend to be deep, as water in the container will settle near the stem of the plant. Access to sunlight can be somewhat limited and the stem or stems of the plant will tend to grow back up toward the sun, often creating a somewhat tangled, unsightly plant. Best results probably happen with a smaller, bush-type variety.

Apparently, a little movement and exercise is good for tomatoes, too. There are several experimental studies that have demonstrated that tomatoes that are exposed to regular brushing or mechanical conditioning grow sturdier stems that resist wind damage or stress better. This brushing prevents stems from elongating too much without any impact on fruit yield or impact on time of fruit production. Experiments also show that seedlings that have been brushed become sturdier and are more likely to survive transplant into the garden.

Chapter 8:
Dealing with Pests and Disease

Knowing something in advance about the potential threats to your tomato plants with respect to insects, animal pests, and disease will go a long way to helping you avoid these threats. Also, some knowledge of these challenges up front will give you skills to observe and identify problems in the tomato garden early. The earlier that you identify a developing problem the better chance you have of overcoming the threat and preventing — or at least limiting — the damage to your developing crop in almost all cases. This is an area where the use of your local Cooperative Extension Service is a wonderful idea. Your local extension service experts will have a good general knowledge of tomato diseases and pests, but they will also be very familiar with specific diseases and pests that are common to your climate and geography. In addition, there are a number of wonderful agricultural Web sites — both USDA-based and Extension Services — which have a wealth of knowledge about identifying and dealing with threats to garden plants. The good thing about growing tomatoes is that because they are such popular garden plants, it is typically a focus area for many agricultural services. *For a list of extension services in your area, Refer to Appendix C.*

As an example, one of these helpful Web sites is the Texas A&M AgriLife Extension Service (**http://texasextension.tamu.edu**). This site has a "Tomato Problem Solver" page that has photographs of a large variety of tomato disorders, which are linked to a description of the culprits that cause the disorders. They also have links to another AgriLife section called "Integrated Pest Management," where you can find suggestions for managing the various insects and diseases described.

General Tips to Encourage Healthy Plants and Fruit

Tomatoes are generally very healthy and resilient plants, but like many garden vegetables are vulnerable to a variety of threats from the time the seeds germinate to the last frost. There are some standard practices that make conditions in your garden more hospitable for disease and insects. Some of these have been mentioned previously, but reinforcing them in this discussion may help emphasize their importance.

- Buy healthy transplants or grow your own seedlings to ensure that you do not start with diseased plants.
- Rotate your tomatoes to different positions in your garden from year to year to avoid a revisit from soil-born pests

from the previous season. Ideally, tomatoes should not be replanted in the same spot until three years have passed.

- Choose a very sunny location. Many fungal-based diseases will be kept in check if plants get enough sunlight.

- Choose varieties that are resistant to plant disease if they are available.

- Use a drip irrigation system to prevent stems and leaves from being wet too often. If drip irrigation is not an option, water early in the day to allow plants to dry out before nightfall.

- Weed around tomato plants and around the periphery of your garden. Weeds provide good homes for a number of insects and disease-causing organisms.

- Remove any plants that show sign of viral disease, as disease will spread readily.

Standard Home-Garden Pesticides

There may be times when you find a need to use pesticide in your garden. While there are some compelling reasons to avoid pesticides whenever possible, there are also situations where diseases and pests can be extremely resistant to organic defenses or deterrents. A limited number of synthetic pesticides are safe and effective for tomato plants and have been approved for use in home gardens. However, keep in mind that tomato plants are pretty productive and resilient and can generally survive the visit of a few aphids. Use pesticides only when you believe the infestation is significant enough to do meaningful damage to your plants or fruit. *For more information on other non-synthetic approaches that can be effective against diseases and pests, see Chapter 9.*

Chemical pesticides for the garden are available in a variety of retail stores, including nurseries, discount stores, and home improvement stores. In general, there are a number of things to be aware of when using chemicals in your garden. First of all, read the labels. While the print can be small, there is always a lot of critical information that you should know. Make sure that whatever you use is approved for use on vegetables and not just for ornamental plants. Some of the pesticides have reasonably long life and you do not want to expose yourself or others to pesticide residues. The label and use instructions will tell you how long you should wait before harvesting any fruit after using the particular pesticide. This is often referred to as the 'preharvest interval.' Make sure you only spray pesticides that are targeted for the pest you are fighting and be sure and target it on the affected plants. Preventative treating with pesticides is not a good idea. Keep spray bottles and dilution equipment for your pesticides separate from fertilizer or watering supplies. Residues can last a long time. In general, care should be used during application as essentially all pesticides should not be ingested and contact with eyes should be avoided.

Malathion: Malathion has also been a standard pesticide in the home garden for decades and is the most commonly used pesticide in the United States. It has broad-based effectiveness against a variety of tomato pests including aphids, mites, and stinkbugs. For tomatoes, malathion has a preharvest interval of three days.

Carbaryl: Carbaryl is one of the most common pesticides used in the home garden and has been sold in the United States for decades, for a wide variety of crops and against a wide variety of insects and organisms. Carbaryl is most often sold under the brand name Sevin®. It is provided in a number of forms, including a non-wettable powder, a liquid concentrate, and pellets. For tomatoes, carbaryl has a preharvest interval of three days.

Pyrethroids: Pyrethroids are a group of synthetic insecticides that are based on the naturally occurring plant chemicals called pyrethrins, which are extracted from chysanthemums. Pyrethroids are effective against a variety of garden pests and can be used at very low application rates. They also tend to degrade in one to two days with exposure to sunlight and atmosphere. This makes them appealing from a health perspective, but limit their long-term effects on pests. They are effective against a wide range of insects. The preharvest interval varies depending on the specific type of pyrethroid used.

Acetamiprid: Acetamiprid has only been on the market since 2009 for home gardens and is marketed under a number of different trade names. It is particularly good for whiteflies and aphids but also used for the tomato fruitworm. Acetamiprid has shown promise for having less impact on naturally occurring parasites and other insect predators than other synthetic pesticides. For tomatoes, acetamiprid has a preharvest interval of seven days.

Insects, Worms, and Strategies to Deter Them

While the typical insects that affect tomatoes will vary somewhat with different climates and different geographies, most insects are common across the United States. This list is not totally comprehensive, but probably covers 90 percent of the pest and disease problems that trouble tomato plants.

With respect to treatment strategies for these tomato threats, this section primarily describes chemical pesticides and fungicides for the garden. There are a number of factors that will determine which approach you should choose to manage your garden. There is an argument for a balanced approach using an organic approach as an initial attempt and only goes to the synthetic pesticide or fungicide approach if the organic approach is found to be lacking. *For descriptions of several organic approaches for managing threats to the garden, see Chapter 9.*

Aphids

Aphids are small white flies that appear in the spring, usually in groups. There are two species of aphids that are most commonly seen on tomatoes — the potato aphid and the green peach aphid. Both are small — about 1/8 inch long — and are typically green or pink. Aphids will feed on leaf sap, but are typically not a direct threat to the tomato fruit. Tomato foliage can tolerate a fairly heavy population of feeding aphids. A severe infestation of aphids should be controlled because a severe attack can kill some of the plant foliage and stunt the overall growth of the plant. Also, aphids are known for carrying and spreading viral diseases that could be more of a threat to the plant. There is also a species called a whitefly that is similar to the aphid, but a little more than half the size. Small numbers of aphids can be ignored because, even though they are present, they do not cause major damage. If the infestation becomes severe, the best pesticide to use for aphids and whiteflies is acetamiprid.

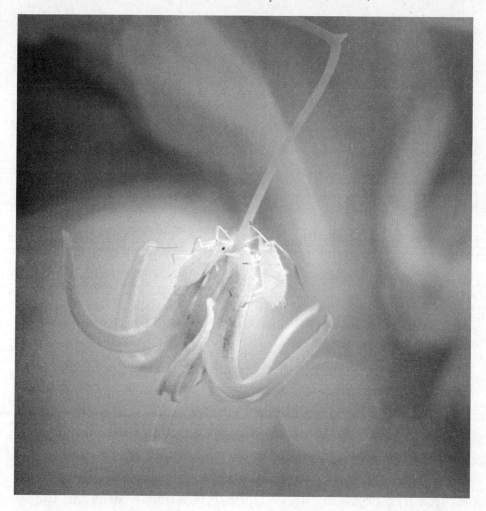

Worms

There are a number of worms that can be either minor nuisances or devastating to the tomato plants. Eggs in the soil that have lasted the winter will hatch in the spring into larvae. The larvae will typically climb above the soil into the plant or stem where they will live and feed on the plant until they drop back into the soil to turn into the pupae. Pupae become moths, which then lay eggs for the next generation. Most worms will have several generations in each growing season.

Cutworms: There are several varieties and colors of cutworms, but the most common is the black cutworm. All tend to be around 1 to 2 inches long. Cutworms do the most damage to new tender seedlings that have recently been transplanted, by cutting off young plants near the ground. A single worm can kill several transplants each night. In this case, if you have had cutworm damage in the past, prevention is better than treatment. Protect young plants by attaching a collar around the base of the tomato plant transplant. The collar can be made of a variety of materials, but should be about 3 inches tall. Some gardeners cut a corrugate toilet paper roll in half or use paper cups with the bottom cut out and use as collars. Press the collar into the soil with about 2 inches remaining above ground around the base of the tomato plant. This will prevent the cutworm from reaching the plant stem.

Hornworms: Hornworms are green caterpillars with white stripes and a distinctive black horn on the tail end. They can be 2 to 3 inches long. The tomato hornworm is very prevalent in the South, but can be found across the United States. They have a variety of natural predators, so they are rarely numerous. Due to their large size, however, they can be fast and voracious feeders. If unnoticed or left unchecked, one or two hornworms can almost completely strip a small plant of its foliage. Because of their camouflaging green color, their presence is often initially detected by the damage they leave behind rather than by seeing the worm itself. In many cases, gardeners can control these worms by picking them off the plant and destroying the larvae. Carbaryl is an effective pesticide if necessary.

Tomato Fruitworm: As indicated by its name, the tomato fruitworm feeds on both the leaves and the fruit — particularly the green fruit — of the tomato plant. This worm will feed on a variety of garden crops and is sometimes called the Corn Earworm.

This worm is not easily identified by its color — it can be green, brown, or black — but does have dark and light stripes running along its body. It grows to about 2 inches long. This worm is not particularly common in home gardens, but if it shows up it can be difficult to manage. This worm is sensitive to carbaryl.

Tomato Pinworm: The tomato pinworm is a small worm, only 1/4 inch long. Like the fruitworm, it is hard to identify by its color because it could be yellow, green, or gray and could have spots depending on the age of the larva. It is usually found in warmer climates, including Florida, California, and Texas because it generally does not survive a cold winter. The identifying characteristic of the presence of the tomato pinworm is tiny boreholes in the fruit or the stem and discoloration of the fruit.

Soil-dwelling Worms: Worms in the soil — including grubs or wireworms — occasionally threaten tomatoes. This happens most often when the garden is grown in an area that was recently covered with sod or grass. The grubs or worms feed on the root structure of the plants, causing damage. If the infestation of these worms is severe enough, the plant will begin to show signs of wilting and poor growth. One trick for finding the presence of grubs or wireworms in the soil is inserting a carrot in the soil close to the tomato plant and checking the carrot for worms every two days. Treatment for these pests is really only done before the growing season begins as you are tilling and preparing the soil. Permethrin, one of the pyrethroids, has efficacy against grubs and wireworms. These worms are only occasionally a threat to tomato plants so treatment is appropriate only if you believe your garden is at high risk for these pests. If you are planning to convert an area from grassy lawn to vegetable garden, kill the grass and till the area as far in advance of planting as possible.

Mites

Mites are a tiny member of the arachnida class that includes spiders and ticks. A few species of mites can be threatening to tomato plants, with spider mites the most common type seen on tomato plants. They are about the size of a grain of salt and have two dark spots on their backs. They tend to congregate on the underside of tomato plant leaves, and once they are established, their signature is a set of silken webs attached to the underside of leaves. They only tend to become a problem with tomato plants during the hottest and driest part of the summer. Spider mites feed on leaves and cause them to develop yellow blotches, and eventually brown and die. Pesticides are usually not effective against mites, and the regular use of some pesticides like carbaryl can create a surge in the spider mite population as a result of killing off their natural predators. Spraying the underside of the leaves with a fine mist of soapy water can reduce their numbers.

Stinkbugs

A stinkbug is a large green or brown bug that is easy to identify because of its flat, shield-shaped body. It is so named because it gives off an unpleasant odor when it is handled or disturbed. Unlike many insect pests, it attacks the tomato fruit rather than the plant stem or foliage. They puncture the fruit most often when it is green, leaving sunken discolored regions. Stinkbugs can be controlled with pyrethroids.

Nematodes

Nematodes are a microscopic roundworm. There are thousands of varieties of nematodes, some of which are beneficial to your garden, as they can be predators to insects or can aid in the decomposition of organic matter in the soil. Your soil is generally loaded with innocuous or beneficial nematodes. A smaller number of nematodes are parasitic to your tomato plants and cause damage and disease. A particular variety of nematode that creates damage to tomato plants is called the root knot nematode. They can damage plants directly or make the plants more susceptible to infection by bacteria, fungi, or viruses. Nematodes live in the soil and burrow into the roots of tomato plants. Roots will be damaged and lateral root growth will be diminished; as a result, overall plant growth will be stunted. Plant foliage will wilt quickly when the soil is dry and will be slow to recover after watering. In many cases, only a few plants in the garden will be affected. The most distinguishing characteristic of plants infected with nematodes can be seen by pulling up the root system. Nematode infection will create a multitude of swollen areas throughout the root system. Your local cooperative extension service can assist you in confirming the identification of nematodes. Nematodes tend to be most prolific in hot, sandy soils, and nematode populations can be controlled somewhat in these soils by adding composted manures or other organic matter. There are no chemical treatments for nematodes that are safe enough for use in the home garden. If your tomato plants are infected with nematodes, you must rely on crop rotation with other vegetables that are not nematode sensitive or choose nematode-resistant tomato cultivars. Fortunately, many cultivars of tomatoes have been developed with nematode resistance.

Animals and Strategies to Deter Them

With the growth and expansion of suburban living, more Americans are living on land that was only recently covered with woods and occupied by a variety of wildlife. Consequently, home gardens are more likely to be challenged by a variety of forest-based animals. Especially in dry periods when green growth in the woods is sparse, gardens become very attractive snack areas for a variety of animals. While you may occasionally come across the animal itself snacking in the garden, it is much more common to find the damaged plants they leave behind. Identifying the culprit is usually easy, based on the prints left behind or on the nature of their droppings. It is easy to find resource sites online with photographs of animal prints and animal droppings that are a good resource for figuring out the identity of the trespasser. One of these sites was created by The Internet Center for Wildlife Damage Management (**http://icwdm.org/inspection**). It offers both a pictorial and a question method for identifying animal droppings and for identifying animal tracks.

Types of animal pests

Deer: Deer populations in the United States have surged over the last 100 years due to a reduction in the populations of their natural predators and to conservation efforts. The population has grown from a low of roughly 500,000 to an estimated 30 million today. In some rural areas, there are up to 40 deer per square mile. Partly just as a result of their sheer numbers, deer are probably the most common threat to vegetable gardens. While tomatoes are probably not their favorite snacking vegetable, they will eat stems, foliage, and green or red fruit if more attractive options are not available. You can most often recognize deer damage by plant branches or even main stems that have been torn off. Deer do not have upper incisors, so they tend to tear plants rather than cut them off cleanly like rabbits do. There are a number of schemes for deterring and delaying the local deer's interest in your garden. However, if there is a healthy population of deer in your area, a barrier fence is the only sure-fire technique for protecting your tomatoes. Deer droppings look like piles of small black pellets.

Rabbits: Rabbits will snack on the young, fresh foliage of almost any new plant in the garden. Once the plants are mature and hardy, rabbits are rarely a problem and there is scant evidence for them eating the tomato fruit. Rabbits do not tend to travel as broadly as deer, so clearing the area around your garden of weeds or high grass will also help to give them less places to nest and hide. The pellets of rabbit droppings are similar in size to deer droppings, but can be brown or black and are generally found in groups of only five to ten.

Squirrels: Squirrels are probably the most difficult animal to eradicate from your garden, due to their agility in climbing, small size, and sheer numbers. They will eat tomato fruit; both green and red. Fortunately, they usually do not eat tomatoes voraciously, so the best strategy is often just to share. If you have an overpopulation of squirrels and sharing is not an option, traps are another approach for ridding your garden of squirrels. As squirrels can be somewhat territorial and it is probably only one or two that are living off your garden, another option to consider is feeding them nuts on a regular basis to give them a better option than your produce.

Birds: Birds, like squirrels, can be very difficult to keep away from your tomato garden. Some believe that bird feeders help by diverting them to another food source. Others believe that feeders just attract more birds to the area. There is no definitive answer on this issue. Often, birds are attracted to tomatoes because of insects that are feeding on the foliage or the fruit. Therefore, insect control is the first line of defense. The only fail-safe option for birds is to use netting. Bird netting is available at a variety of garden and home improvement stores. Depending on the size of your tomato crop, the netting can be applied in sheets across multiple plants or cut in smaller squares to apply over individual plants.

Alarms and deterrents

While fencing always works the best for both rabbits and deer, there are some other options for those who want to avoid putting up a fence. These deterrents will work to varying degrees. Many will work for a short period of time before the animal becomes accustomed to the deterrent and decides that the snacks are worth the inconvenience. There are a number of deterrents for deer that use motion sensors to sense the deer and then activate something to chase them away. Radios are sometimes effective, especially tuning the station to a talk show. Lights can also work, as many animals will feed at dusk and dawn. Sprinklers can also be hooked up with a motion sensor switch to turn on and off and scare deer and rabbits.

There are a number of materials that you can place in and around the garden to discourage or deter rabbits and deer from venturing into your garden. These are based on the animals being repelled by the odor of the agent. Coyote urine is sold in many garden shops for this purpose. The typical strategy is to pour the urine into small plastic containers with tiny holes in the tops, so the animals can easily detect the urine without the containers being washed away by rains. These containers can be placed around the periphery of the garden and at a couple of spots within the garden. Other repellents based on odor include human hair and mothballs.

The other category of repellents works based on the animal's sense of taste. For example; dusting plants directly with fine particles of cayenne pepper. This will deter most animals and some insect pests, but when the plants become large and leafy, it becomes increasingly difficult to cover all the leaves and to re-cover the leaves after a rain. There are a number of commercial materials you can find in home and garden stores or on-line, often based on ammonia or sulfur chemistries, which are developed as specific repellents for deer and rabbits. No repellent will continuously repel all deer for a long period of time. If you choose to use repellents, you should rotate different ones and reapply on a regular basis. Also, repellents should be used early in the season before damage to your plants has occurred. Once the deer have discovered your crop and become accustomed to eating them, they are hard to discourage.

Fencing and netting

There are a number of approaches for effective fencing for deer and rabbits. The choice depends on the size of your garden, whether you want a permanent structure or one that you can remove every season, and how much you want to invest. As with repellent strategies, fences should be put up before the growing season is underway and before animals have discovered the garden and become accustomed to the fresh snacks. Deer can jump to heights of up to 8 feet, so a fence should be 7 to 8 feet high to effectively deter deer. Another strategy is to build the fence shorter but wider, as jumping over longer distances reduces the height they can reach. One approach based on this idea is to build the fence slanted outward at a 45-degree angle. In all cases, the fence should not be constructed close to the edge of the woods as that would make it more likely that the deer might accidently run into the fence and damage it. Fences can be constructed from a variety of materials. For aesthetic reasons, many growers prefer to use fencing materials that can be easily constructed, deconstructed, and stored for the winter. Simple but effective deer fences can be built using treated posts and twine stretched between the posts at roughly 10- to 20-inch intervals. Another good approach that keeps out both rabbits and deer is the use of netting. Both of these approaches are fairly inconspicuous and can blend in with the garden and other landscaping fairly well. Seven-foot-high netting for this purpose is available at many nurseries or home and garden stores. Most of the netting will come with galvanized stakes that should be used to push the netting into the ground every several feet to keep rabbits and other small animals out of the garden. Posts can be placed at pretty wide spacings, as the netting puts very little stress on the posts. In both of these examples, some bright streamers should be tied to the fence about 4 feet off the ground to make the fence more visible to the deer.

Electric fences also can be very effective in keeping deer away from your vegetable plants. They can be erected in multiple configurations with one or more wires strung at different heights. They can be powered from an AC supplied power charger or, if power is not available close to the garden, a solar-powered or DC battery-powered charger. The fences provide a low-amperage, high-voltage charge that will deter deer and rabbits. Deer will learn quickly to avoid the fence and the area it surrounds. Be sure and use caution with electric fences in areas where other people and especially children — are around. Always be sure and put up signs to warn of the electrified fence.

Standard Home Garden Fungicides and Bactericides

There are a number of chemistries that are sold for home garden use that have efficacy against some of the bacteria and fungi that can cause diseases in tomato plants. Unlike pesticides for tomatoes, many of these must be used in a preventative fashion or minimally at the very first sign of infection. If plants are already severely diseased, the fungicide will not provide a cure. The best approach is to remove all affected foliage completely and to spray the remaining healthy leaves with the fungicide. Application should be repeated regularly per the label directions and should always be repeated after a rain. As with pesticides, pay close attention to label instructions regarding pre harvest intervals.

Copper Sulfate Spray or Dust: This is used on tomatoes to control early and late blight, and a variety of leaf spots. It has bactericidal, fungicidal, and some insecticidal properties. Copper sulfate has a one-day pre-harvest interval for tomatoes.

Chlorothalonil: This is a broad-spectrum fungicide that is often used on tomatoes and sold under the brand names Bravo, Echo, and Daconil. It is appropriate for a variety of leaf spots and blights and is sometimes mixed with copper sulfate. It is indicated to have no pre-harvest interval for tomatoes.

Mancozeb with Zinc: This is a fungicide used to control a variety of leaf spots and blights. It is sold under a number of brand names including Dithane, Manzeb, and Nemispot. It has a pre-harvest interval of five days for tomatoes.

Tomato Diseases and Strategies

Disease is probably the largest threat to growing tomatoes. While diseases are often reasonably rare, an infection not quickly identified and managed can destroy an entire crop. Your tomato garden can go for years without issue, often giving many home gardeners a sense of complacency. However, once a disease entrenches itself, it can be incredibly difficult to eradicate. Commercial growers will often pre-treat seedlings or soil to guard against disease if they have had previous infections or if a particular infection is common in their area. Home gardeners rarely need to go to these lengths. For almost all types of disease, there are three primary strategies for avoiding disease.

- Choose reputable vendors for healthy seeds and healthy seedlings.

- Rotate tomato plants to different sections of the garden to avoid organisms that overwinter in the soil.

- Choose disease-resistant cultivars.

The home gardener has a large number of hybrid tomatoes from which to choose that have been bred over the years specifically for disease resistance. This does not mean that the plants will not become infected with the specified organism or is immune to the disease. It does mean that the infection, if it occurs, will typically have much less impact on the plant and the plant will survive through fruit harvest. A naming system has been developed for denoting the type of resistance tomatoes have. Seed packages are generally labeled with V, F, N, T, A, S or a combination of these. These letters have the following meanings for tomato seeds:

V — Resistance to **Verticillium**

F — Resistance to **Fusarium**

N — Resistance to **Nematodes**

T — Resistance to **Tobacco Mosaic Virus**

A — Resistance to Early Blight caused by **Alternaria fungus**

S — Resistance to **Stemphylium Gray Leaf Spot**

This is one area where there are an abundance of online resources to aid in identification and treatment of tomato plant diseases. Many sites are linked to specific state cooperative extension services or state universities and have general information as well as information targeted at diseases common in the local geography and climate. You will often find detailed descriptions of the disease and its symptoms as well as pictures with examples of diseased plants that you can compare your crop to. There is information targeted for both commercial farmers as well as home gardeners in the area. They also will often have timely information about outbreaks of particular agricultural diseases in the local area in recent years. One example is a chart compiled by Cornell University Plant Pathology Department that lists tomato diseases and identifies tomato cultivars that are resistant to these diseases and seed sources for these particular cultivars. (**http://vegetablemdonline.ppath.cornell.edu/Tables/TomatoTable.html**)

Bacterial diseases

In general, the bacterial diseases of most plants tend to be carried in and transmitted from the seed. For this reason, bacterial-based tomato plant diseases are systemic. This means the bacteria will be transported to the plant through the plant vascular system. Therefore the disease can affect the entire plant and fruit and be very difficult to treat. If you buy seeds from reliable, well-known sources, you are less likely to have exposure to bacterial based tomato plant diseases. If you choose to collect seeds, be sure to collect seeds from healthy plants that have been prepared and stored carefully. *For more information on proper techniques for saving seeds, see Chapter 11.*

One of the difficulties in dealing with bacterial-based plant diseases is the symptoms are broad-based and non-specific, which makes the specific disease difficult to diagnose. The only definitive data is a microbiological test, which some extension services are willing and able to do for you. The other primary difficulty is that chemical treatment only works when the plant is young and before disease symptoms are present. As a consequence, if you find that your plants are infected, your only recourse is to destroy the plant and treat the soil and/or next season's seedlings before planting. If you suspect that your tomato plants have been infected with a bacterial-based disease, avoid planting tomato plants in that same area for at least two years. There are three main types of tomato plant diseases caused by bacteria:

Bacterial Canker: Bacterial canker is a reasonably rare disease in home gardens, but can be so destructive and contagious that it can wipe out an entire tomato crop. The primary symptoms of the disease are wilting, curling, and eventually browning of the leaves. Often, plants symptoms will at first appear on only one side of the plant or on one side of a leaf as only part of the vascular system is affected initially. Despite the fact that the disease is born in the seed, the tomato plant may not begin to show signs of disease until after the plant has flowered. As the plant matures, signs of the disease may show up inside the fruit as discolored spots. If diseased plants are not removed from the garden soon, bacteria will colonize on the surface of leaves and then spread to the surface of other plants. Damage may then begin to show up on the surface of green fruit.

Bacterial Spot: Bacterial spot manifests itself as small, irregular dark lesions on the tomato leaf and stem that eventually result in larger yellowing of the tomato plant leaves. On fruit, the signs of infection are first tiny dark spots that eventually become raised and can grow to 1/4 inch in diameter. Green pepper plants are also vulnerable to this bacterium and will develop similar spots.

Moist weather, splashing rains, or overhead irrigation in combination with warm temperatures create good conditions for the spread of this disease.

Bacterial Speck: Bacterial speck disease results in similar lesions to bacterial spot on tomato plant leaves. Particularly important for this disease is the previously mentioned advice not to replant tomato plants in the same garden space each season. This is because of evidence that the bacteria responsible for this disease can overwinter in the soil or on plant material in the compost pile. This bacterial disease is more comfortable in cooler temperatures than the bacterial spot or canker; therefore it is more common in northern climates.

Tomato Tidbits

Salicylic acid — a compound very similar to aspirin — has been found to be produced in plants as a defensive response when disease or pests threaten; sort of a plant immune response. Several groups have experimented with spraying tomato plants with a solution of aspirin to bolster the plant defenses against disease. A chemical company has also produced a material that is related to salicylic acid and is marketing it as Actigard for the treatment of bacterial leaf diseases in tomatoes, as well as a variety of other plant diseases.

Fungal diseases

Fungal diseases are the most common of the tomato plant diseases. Tomato fungal diseases are characterized as either blight or wilt. Airborne spores — which need moist or wet conditions to thrive — spread blight diseases from plant to plant. Wilt diseases are caused by fungal infection in the vascular system of the plant rather than topical infection. Crop rotation is a key strategy for managing against fungal diseases; both blight and wilt. Many fungi are very hardy, so if fungal diseases affect your plants, you should strive to avoid planting tomatoes again in this spot for at least three years. Overhead sprinkling encourages fungal blight spread, and if fungal disease is an issue in your tomato garden, drip irrigation will be a definite benefit. As leaves become affected by blight, it is best to carefully remove affected foliage and bury it. If you have an active compost pile, the heat from composting organic matter will destroy fungus. Following are the many fungal diseases that can affect you tomato garden:

Early Blight: This disease is caused by the fungus, *Alternaria solani*, and usually begins after the first fruit is set. It most often starts on the lower leaves of the plant and is relatively easy to identify. Large, dark brown or black spots develop on the leaves, which include a series of concentric rings that resemble a target. The leaves will eventually turn yellow around these target spots and die. Spots can also appear on the stems and on the fruit of the tomato plants. This fungus can also affect potato plants and eggplant vines. Like most fungal diseases, the fungus spreads most rapidly in warm, moist weather and is more common later in the growing season. This fungus is very hardy, and will last over the winter on old tomato vines and in weeds for several years.

Late Blight: The fungus *Phytophthora infestans* causes this disease. It is the same fungus that was responsible for the great potato famine in Ireland in the mid 1800s. In tomatoes, this blight is favored when the weather is humid or moist and warm, but not hot (around 85 degrees Fahrenheit). Dark green or black spots begin forming at the leaf edge and spread. Spots will also develop on the tomato fruit.

Septoria Blight: The fungus *Septoria lycopersici* causes Septoria blight, which is distinguished by small round spots with darker edges and tiny black dots throughout the spot. When the fungal spots become numerous, the leaves finally turn yellow and drop. Lower leaves are usually affected first, so you often have a chance to remove affected foliage as soon as detected to protect upper leaves. This fungus does not directly affect fruit, but if left unchecked the plant will eventually die. This fungus is hardy and will survive the winter in plant refuse or weeds.

There are two primary wilt diseases that are caused by fungal organisms. The wilt diseases are more difficult to treat than the blight diseases as a result of being carried through the vascular system of the plant. For both of these wilt diseases, many tomato hybrids have been developed that are resistant. Both of the funguses that cause these wilt diseases are very hardy and can survive in the soil for up to eight years, so crop rotation is particularly important.

Fusarium Wilt: This is caused by the fungus, *Fusarium oxysporum*, and is a common fungus in tomato gardens. It is encouraged by warm soil temperatures, greater than 80 degrees Fahrenheit, and by low soil pH. It is most common in southern gardens and less common in the northern half of the United States. It infects the plant through the roots using the plant vascular system. Usually the first sign of infection is yellowing of the lower leaves of one branch of the plant. If the stem is cut, you will find a dark brown discoloration of the inner vascular system of the plant. If the disease is left untreated it will progress up the stem, first affecting only one side of the plant, but eventually killing the plant. This fungus can also affect relatives of the tomato plant, including potatoes, eggplants, and peppers.

Verticillium Wilt: This disease is caused by the fungi *Verticillium albo-atrum* and *Verticillium dahliae*. The disease symptoms are almost indistinguishable from the Fusarium wilt. Unlike the Fusarium fungus, Verticillium is favored in cooler climates with soil temperatures around 75 degrees Fahrenheit and more neutral pH's.

Gray Leaf Spot: The fungus *Stemphylium solani* causes this disease. It manifests itself as brown or black spots, which occur on both old and young leaves. The spots will eventually expand and the leaf will turn yellow and die. Like many fungal diseases, overhead sprinkling of water and warm, wet climates encourage it. There are several hybrid tomato cultivars that have resistance to this fungal disease.

Gray Mold, Leaf Mold, and Powdery Mildew: These mold diseases are caused by a variety of fungi. They are found in the garden occasionally but are more common in greenhouse tomatoes. All require very high humidity to survive. You can reduce the likelihood of these diseases by planting tomato plants with sufficient spacing in sunny areas and exercising adequate pruning to remove foliage and allow good air circulation. As these diseases are often caused by a variety of fungi, there are no tomato cultivars that offer good resistance to these diseases. In many of these diseases, the tomato fruit are either unaffected or if spots develop they are only superficial.

Damping Off: Damping off is a somewhat general term, referring to the death of seedlings either just before or just after emergence from the soil. In most cases, once the plant has two or three sets of leaves, it is no longer susceptible to damping off. The disease can be caused by a number of different species of fungus and more often occurs in cool, wet soils. If you are planting seeds inside, then planting medium or sterilized soil should prevent problems with damping off. If you plant seeds directly in the garden, seeds can be treated with a fungicide if damping off has been a problem in your garden.

Viral diseases

Tomato diseases caused by viruses probably pose the least threat to the home gardener, much less than diseases caused by fungi. The tomato seed rarely carries viral diseases. In general, insects or human contact spread these diseases. These viral wilt diseases are essentially impossible to treat effectively, so diseased plants should be removed from the garden as soon as possible. The following is a list of the most common virus-caused tomato diseases.

Tobacco Mosaic Virus: This virus is one of the most stable of all viruses, able to survive on dry plant material for up to 100 years. Humans most often spread it, but this virus can occasionally be seed-borne. Tobacco Mosaic Virus may be present in tobacco products, so some discourage smoking in or near the garden. This disease tends to be more common in the southern part of the United States. It is often identified by the characteristic light and dark green mottled pattern, which gave the virus its name. Most often, the fruit on the plant is not affected but the yield will be significantly reduced as the foliage suffers. There are a variety of different strains of Tobacco Mosaic Virus, so specific plant symptoms can vary. There are a number of tomato cultivars that are resistant to this virus.

Cucumber Mosaic Virus: Unlike the Tobacco Mosaic Virus, this virus is not spread by seeds or human contact. It is not a particularly stable virus and will not overwinter in soil or plant refuse. Aphids carrying the virus from other locations are largely responsible for the spread of Cucumber Mosaic Virus. The primary symptom of this virus is a set of leaves with the shape of thin blades of grass. There have been no hybrids developed with resistance to this virus.

Spotted Wilt Virus: This virus is reasonably rare in outside home gardens and is characterized by orange spots on middle or lower leaves and stems. The virus is transmitted by the larval form of the thrip, which is a tiny winged insect that poses little threat to tomato plants. It can be found in soil and is best avoided by ensuring your purchased transplants are healthy and come from a reliable source.

Other diseases

There are a number of other tomato plant diseases or conditions not associated with infection by organisms, but instead are a result of difficult growing conditions or insufficient nutrients:

Blossom End Rot: Blossom end rot is a common tomato disease found in many gardens. It is characterized by a large spot on the bottom end of the fruit that looks water-saturated in green fruit and black or dark brown in red fruit. It is caused by a calcium deficiency in the fruit. A soil test can tell you whether low calcium levels in the soil cause the calcium deficiency. If so, add limestone (calcium carbonate) when soil pH is below 6; add gypsum, which is a mineral version of calcium sulfate, when soil pH is above 6. Most often, blossom end rot is not related to soil chemistry but is a consequence of fluctuations in water supply. Tomato plants do not manage drought conditions well. The best way to avoid blossom end rot is to water on a regular basis and to use a mulch to prevent the soil from evaporating so quickly during dry periods.

Some advocate calcium-based sprays for the leaves but these do not work as the calcium must be adsorbed through the roots.

Catfacing: This term describes misshapen fruit, especially on the bottom end, that often has multiple lobes and scars. It is caused by damage to the blossoms by cool temperatures. Extended periods with temperatures at 60 to 65 degrees Fahrenheit or nighttime temperatures in the 50s when the plant is forming blooms can cause catfacing. In most climates, this is more common with early fruit.

Fruit Cracking: When tomato fruit is ripening during hot and rainy weather, the stem end of the fruit will often develop rough, dark, and sometimes deep cracks. The cracks are caused by too rapid uptake of water into the fruit after a hot, dry period. These cracks can go around the tomato end or extend in a radial pattern from the stem. Mulching and regular watering can mitigate this problem. In addition, if the weather in your area encourages cracking, there are several crack-resistant tomato varieties.

Sunscald: Sun scald is a yellow or white area on the side of the fruit most exposed to the hot sun. This happens most often as a result of insufficient foliage to shade the fruit. Over-aggressive pruning or insufficient nutrients are often responsible for inadequate foliage. This condition can be encouraged by hot, sunny weather. The scalded spots can also be potential sites for bacterial or fungal infection.

Chapter 9:
Organic Tomato Gardening

Organic gardening has seen a significant increase in popularity over the last decade. It is now pretty common to find an organic section with a wide selection of organic fresh vegetables in almost every grocery store. Also, local markets focusing on organic vegetables spring up regularly in the growing season in many communities. While organically managed farm land still represents only about 1 percent of all farmland worldwide, it is estimated that commercial acreage dedicated to growing organic vegetables has increased by about 20 percent every year during the last decade. This is largely due to growers discovering that the market will pay about a 20 to 30 percent premium for organically grown vegetables. For the home gardener, the fundamentals of organic gardening — avoiding synthetic chemicals and recycling waste — make sense to most growers. As tomato plants tend to be reasonably hardy and resistant to most pests and disease, growing tomatoes organically is a very reasonable objective. While it is probably not realistic to expect all home tomato growers to go pure organic, it does make sense to try and incorporate many of the organic gardening principles into your tomato garden.

Why Organic

Definition of organic

In the United States, "organic" has become a significant marketing label for commercial vegetable crops over the last decade. The National Organic Program is part of the USDA and is responsible for ensuring that commercial growers who label their produce as organic meet strict guidelines and are certified by an accredited third party. The major requirements for commercial growers are: They cannot use synthetic fertilizers, synthetic pesticides, synthetic fungicides, synthetic herbicides, or any genetically modified seeds or organisms. For the home garden, while compliance to the details of the National Organic Program instructions is obviously not required, the basic objectives are essentially the same. Composting and using various forms of composted organic material to replace fertilizer is an important component. Natural, non-synthetic strategies to fight tomato pests, diseases, and weeds are the other key components. Genetically modified seeds or organisms are not yet a factor for the home tomato gardener.

Health benefits

Consumers tend to believe that organic vegetables are healthier and more flavorful. Substantive health data has not yet been developed, but research in this area continues. Experimental trials have demonstrated an increase in key vitamins and antioxidants in many organic vegetables and a lower level of agricultural chemical residues. Several experimental studies have been carried out to answer the question of whether organically grown tomatoes can offer health benefits. In one study at the University of California, Davis, researchers found that organic tomatoes had almost double the level of flavonoids as regularly grown tomatoes. Flavonoids are a natural plant metabolite that serves as a pigment in the tomato skin and also has some protective properties for the tomato against ultraviolet light damage and is a deterrent against some insect predators. Flavonoids have antioxidant and anti-inflammatory properties and may play a role in reducing cancer and cardiovascular disease. Research in this area is limited, but with the increased interest in organic in the marketplace, future studies are planned. Some scientists believe there are more healthy tomato components yet to be discovered. Many theorize that the increase in nutrients is likely linked to the use of composted organic fertilizers rather than synthetic fertilizers. Synthetic fertilizers tend to make soluble nitrogen immediately available to the plant in large doses. The more slow and steady delivery of nitrogen via the decomposition of organic matter may create a more balanced growth environment that favors fruit value rather than foliage. Another theory for the increased level of flavonoids in organically grown tomatoes is the idea that the total reliance on organic matter for nitrogen versus adding nitrogen directly with synthetic fertilizer stresses the plant. This stress on the plant provokes defense mechanisms on the part of the tomato plant, which encourage the production of defense compounds, one of which is the flavonoids. This could be viewed analogous to the development of healthier humans by the stress that exercise puts on our bodies.

Environmental benefits

The environmental benefits of organic farming or gardening can be somewhat complex, but includes several factors that appeal to the more environmentally conscious gardeners.

Reduced chemical residues and run-off is probably the most clear and obvious environmental benefit of growing organic. Some of the chemicals available for use in the garden — such as pesticides, fungicides or those used for weed control — persist for some time or have degradation products that will persist. These chemicals can last on the plant foliage or in the soil and pose a potential threat to children or pets. Also, chemical residues can eventually wash off into local waterways. In addition, many of these agents can have unintended impacts on other parts of your garden ecosystem. This can be direct toxic impact on beneficial organisms or killing off predators that might be controlling the population of threatening organisms to the garden.

In addition, both the production and the use of synthetic fertilizers also pose a pretty significant negative environmental impact. On the production side, making synthetic fertilizer is very energy intensive. It is estimated that fertilizer production consumes about 5 percent of the world's natural gas production. The other environmental issue associated with using synthetic fertilizer in agriculture is the ease with which excess nitrogen in the soil is leached out and runs off into streams or ground water. Essentially, the excess nitrogen poisons lakes by the encouragement of the growth of algae, which when produced in excess depletes the water of oxygen and starves out fish and other organisms.

Another environmental benefit of organic gardening is less water use in your garden. Often, adding organic matter to your soil will improve the efficiency of water use in the soil, particularly if your soil is naturally sandy. And the addition of generous organic mulch to your garden soil will both reduce evaporative water loss and soil erosion.

Other benefits

While few gardeners embark on an organic approach for their gardens with the intent to save money, it can work out to be a cost-effective approach. Garden pesticides, fungicides, and herbicides are surprisingly expensive, and reducing or eliminating their use can certainly save money. In addition, many types of organic matter can be recovered from your own home, lawn, and garden. These might include raked straw and leaves, grass clippings, ash from wood fires, food waste, or shredded newspapers. You can also find neighbors with such materials who are often happy to let you take these materials off their hands. Organic matter can also be acquired free of charge from local companies or municipalities that produce them as by-products. Some examples of these materials are used coffee grounds from coffee shops, sawdust from lumber yards or home-improvement stores, shredded branches and trees from city maintenance departments, and poultry or horse manure from local farms.

CASE STUDY: NEW TECHNOLOGY IN FERTILIZING TOMATOES

Louis H. Elwell, III
President of Bio Soil™ Enhancers, Inc
www.miracle-microbes.com
www.biosoilenhancers.com

CLASSIFIED CASE STUDIES
directly from the experts

Another approach for feeding the soil and mitigating disease risk in an organic fashion has been developed at Michigan State University and is being marketed by the company Bio Soil™ Enhancers. Louis Elwell, president of the company, talks about new technology in fertilizing tomatoes.

The new approach to fertilizing tomatoes is basically a formulation of specially selected microbes that are added to the soil. These microbes have several important functions. Most importantly, they are designed to fix nitrogen from the air into a form that plants can take up as nutrients. Secondly, these microbes compete with pathogenic microbes in the soil and reduce the likelihood of plant disease. Finally, some of the microbes act to produce metabolites that stimulate root and plant growth. These microbes essentially allow nutrients in the air and soil to become bio-available for plants to use without the need for additional petrochemical-based fertilizers. "This approach is applicable to a variety of grain and vegetable crops as well as lawns," Elwell said. "It offers an amazing opportunity to increase world food supplies. It also promises an important reduction in synthetic fertilizer use."

The Bio Soil team has a special organic formulation specifically designed for growing tomatoes. The results using the product on tomatoes are especially impressive. "In a greenhouse setting, the use of the Bio Soil microbes increased the yield of tomato plants by 400 percent over conventional fertilizers alone," Elwell said. "The average size of the tomatoes increased by 88 percent using the Bio Soil microbes." In addition, the tomatoes had a faster germination rate and flowered more quickly when using the Bio Soil microbes.

The Bio Soil formulation also contains humates and plant micronutrients. Humates are the product of organic matter degradation and provide a food supply for the microbes. According to Elwell, using Bio Soil microbes will cost less than conventional synthetic fertilizers. The company is also currently in the process of applying for organic certification for their formulations.

Soil Maintenance

A fundamental tenet of organic gardening is the creation of healthy, well-structured soil with sufficient nitrogen-rich nutrients — without using synthetic fertilizers. Many of the approaches described here are important for growing tomatoes whether you have decided to grow organically or not. These strategies — including cover crops and composting — not only provide nitrogen and other nutrients to the soil but they also improve the soil structure. For most soils, the structure improvement reduces the soil density and porosity so air, moisture, and nutrients are able to easily reach the roots. When gardening organically — without using synthetic fertilizers — cover crops and composting are critical and serve as the primary mechanism for providing nitrogen for the tomato plants.

Cover crops

A very useful approach that applies to home growers in general — but can be critically important for organic tomato gardeners — is planting winter cover crops. Cover crops are planted not for harvest but to improve the soil, reduce erosion in winter rains, and to reduce weeds. Cover crops can be tilled back into the garden soil or they can be cut and allowed to dry on the surface to provide mulch around your tomato crop. The choice to till in or mow the cover crop is somewhat of a toss-up. If early tomatoes are a primary objective, the best option is to till in the winter cover crop, as the cut cover crop that becomes mulch will keep the soil cooler in the spring. On the other hand, mowing the cover crop and not tilling the soil in the spring before planting helps to maintain soil structure and organic matter and helps to reduce weeds. Allowing for the slower decomposition of the cover crop on the surface may even out the delivery of nitrogen to the soil over the growing season. In most areas of the United States, cover crops are planted in the fall, grown over the winter, and tilled or cut in the early spring. In some warmer climates, like southern Florida and southern California, cover crops are typically grown in the summer when it is too hot for tomato plants. Some gardeners will also choose to grow cover crops around their tomato plants during the growing season; often called "living mulches." There are multiple options for growing living mulch in the rows between your tomato plants with clover or rye as the most common. The living mulch cover crop will suppress weeds by competing with weed seeds for light, moisture, and nutrients. You will need to perform some cultivation or tilling between the tomato plants and the cover crop to prevent the cover crop from using valuable moisture and nutrients intended for the tomato plants.

Nutrient addition and retention in the soil is a primary benefit of growing a cover crop. Legume crops in particular are able to capture nitrogen from the atmosphere and convert or fix it into the soil in the form of ammonia or nitrates. Legume plants accomplish this nitrogen fixation by cooperating with a species of bacteria (Rhizobium) in the soil in a mutually beneficial or symbiotic relationship. The plant provides nutrients, energy, and shelter for the bacteria; the bacteria convert the nitrogen gas in the atmosphere and soil into ammonia. Nitrogen in the form of a gas is useless to the plant, but in the form of ammonia can be absorbed and metabolized. Some examples of legume cover crops are clover, winter pea, alfalfa, and soybeans. Non-legume plants do not fix nitrogen, but they do absorb nitrogen from the soil and essentially store it in the plant stem and foliage. This holds the nitrogen and helps prevent it from being leached out of the soil by winter rains. The non-legume plants also provide organic matter or biomass, which act to improve the structure of the soil. In the early spring, non-legume cover crops can be tilled into the soil to degrade and provide organic matter and some nitrogen for your tomato crop. The roots of cover crops — both legumes and non-legumes — also benefit the soil by keeping it more porous and open.

In many areas of the country — especially in the Southeast — the winter months have the highest levels of rainfall. This rainfall can contribute to significant soil erosion on barren soil. It will also cause leaching of soil nutrients from the soil, which ultimately run off into lower-lying areas and streams. In some cases, the cover crop will be mowed or cut rather than tilled in the spring, and the residue will be left on the garden soil. This residue will also limit erosion from early spring rains. Cover crops also have an impact on limiting weeds in the garden. Cover crops can work by competing with weeds for soil moisture, nutrients, and sunlight. In addition, cover crops have been demonstrated to emit substances that inhibit weed seed germination and growth in some cases. This effect is called allelopathy. Fortunately, tomato seeds and seedlings are very resistant to this effect, and will flourish while weeds struggle.

The choice of cover crop will partly depend on your local climate; it will also depend on whether you intend to till the cover crop in to add nutrients or you want to cut it down to dry in place and act as a mulch. These are some of the most common cover crops you might consider for the tomato garden:

Clover: Clover is one of the legume-type cover crops that, with the help of soil bacteria, fixes nitrogen from the atmosphere into the soil. There are several types of clover commonly used for cover crops, including red clover and crimson clover. Clovers typically grow 20 to 40 inches tall and are reasonably tolerant to winter weather. Clovers tend to attract insects, some of which are beneficial to tomatoes, but they may also encourage root-knot nematodes, which can be destructive to tomatoes.

Hairy Vetch: Hairy vetch is a vine-producing legume that works well as a cover crop with tomatoes as well as other warm weather vegetables. It produces purple flowers, which tend to attract beneficial insects like ladybugs and some beetles. Hairy vetch can be mowed down, dried in place, and used as mulch or be tilled into the garden. The cover crop seed should be planted from late August to mid October, depending on your climate. As it is a legume, it contributes a good amount of nitrogen to the soil, but also delivers potassium, phosphorous, and other micronutrients. Hairy vetch will form a thick mat across the garden soil and consequently acts as an effective erosion control medium as well. Hairy vetch can be mowed before planting the tomato transplants or tilled into the garden several weeks before transplanting to give time for the foliage to begin decomposition. In some situations, hairy vetch can provide a haven for some insects pests, so this early cutting or tilling will give time for them to decline before planting transplants.

Rye: Annual rye is a hardy non-legume cover crop that is grown in almost all climates in the United States. Seeds are sown in the late fall and grow through the winter. It should be mowed and left on the surface as mulch or mowed and tilled into the soil. This should be done at least three weeks before putting tomato transplants into the garden. The rye should be tilled after the plant has flowered, as it will regrow if it is mowed earlier. Rye is a good crop for scavenging nitrogen from the soil. This prevents the nitrogen remaining in the soil after the tomato-growing season from being washed away with winter rains. The nitrogen is then returned to the soil when the rye is tilled into the soil in the spring. The rye crop essentially acts as a safe storage device to protect and conserve nitrogen over the winter. However, because it is not a legume, it will not deliver new nitrogen to the soil the way that clover, hairy vetch, or other legumes will. As rye grass grows fast and tall, it does create a lot of biomass or organic matter that can act to provide useful mulch when mowed or provide soil structure improvements when tilled in. Finally, rye grass roots have been demonstrated to have a particularly active allelopathic effect, discouraging weed seed germination and growth for several weeks after it is mowed.

Austrian Winter Peas: The Austrian winter pea is a legume with a low, vine-type structure that produces purplish flowers and then pods with dark-colored seeds. It can be grown over the winter in most areas of the United States, except in areas where there are long periods of sub-zero winter weather. Like most other winter crops, it is planted in September or October, depending on the local latitude and climate. This crop is a favorite of deer, however, so it may attract them to your garden.

In some cases, gardeners choose to plant a mix of cover crop seed to attempt to get a balance of benefits. A good strategy is the combination of a fast-growing non-legume, such as rye grass, with a nitrogen-fixing legume, such as hairy vetch or clover. In most cases, seeds are broadcast together in the fall. This kind of combination provides for the strong biomass production of the faster-growing, taller rye grass with the nitrogen-fixing performance of the legume. Finally, cover crops — like tomatoes — should be managed through crop rotation. Varying the cover crop to avoid planting the same crop year after year will give some diversity to the nutrients provided to the soil and also reduce the incidence of disease and insect pests.

Composting

Compost is partially decomposed organic matter. It is typically black and crumbly and has an earthy aroma. It is created from the biological process of organisms in the soil working on the organic matter to degrade and decompose it. The end result of this degradation is a material called humus, which is dark brown and powdery and survives in the soil indefinitely. The decomposition process that happens in a compost pile is similar to what happens naturally on the forest floor, but it happens more quickly in the compost pile as conditions are controlled and adjusted so the microorganisms can work most efficiently. Composting not only produces a wonderful source of organic matter and nutrients for your tomato garden, but it also provides a cost-effective and environmentally healthy approach for getting rid of lawn and garden waste, which would otherwise require hauling off. Composting also allows you to recycle a lot of home and garden waste that could otherwise end up in landfills, including food waste, grass and shrub clippings, newspaper, and other paper waste.

There are several characteristics that make for a good compost pile. A good compost pile must contain the right mix of organic material to properly balance the ratio of carbon to nitrogen in the compost. First, a brief chemistry lesson: All organic material derived from plants and animals contains carbon and nitrogen. Carbon is the major component of cellulose, which gives grasses and woody materials their structure and strength. Nitrogen is a key component of proteins, DNA, and other plant and animal cell components. Some organic materials — like leaves and wood chips — are high in carbon with carbon to nitrogen ratios of at least 100 to 1. Other organic materials — like poultry manure or fishmeal — are more nitrogen rich and have a carbon to nitrogen ratio of roughly 5 or 10 to 1. The best compost pile contains a mix of organic material that ends up with a ratio of carbon to nitrogen of about 30 to 1. This gives microorganisms the best material to work with for the most efficient decomposition. There are multiple extension service resources and Web sites that provide estimates of nitrogen content for a variety of organic matter you might wish to add to your compost pile. One way to characterize composting materials is as high nitrogen materials, green materials, or brown materials. A good standard is to target the composition to be 1/3 high-nitrogen materials (legumes or manure), 1/3 "green" materials (grass clippings or coffee grounds), and 1/3 "brown" materials (wood chips or sawdust).

So, what materials can be added to the compost pile? Composting is not an exact science and essentially anything that is derived from plants or animals can be composted. There are some limitations, as some materials may decompose very slowly, attract animal pests, or enhance the risk of spreading disease:

High nitrogen materials: These materials are important, as they provide the nitrogen that microorganisms need in the decomposition process. They typically have carbon to nitrogen ratios ranging from 6 to 1 up to 20 to 1. Animal manures are one of the most common high-nitrogen materials used. The amount of nitrogen in the manure varies significantly with different animals. Chicken manure is the most rich in nitrogen, followed by manure from pigs, cows, and then horses. Poultry manure can have two to three times the amount of nitrogen than horse manure or cow manure. Therefore, the proportion of poultry manure used should drop to roughly half the 1/3 target described above. Another high-nitrogen option is alfalfa hay, which generally has a carbon to nitrogen ratio of 13 to 1. Alfalfa hay is a popular forage material for horses, so it is often available from stables or farming supply vendors.

Green compost materials: Green compost materials fall in the carbon to nitrogen ratio range of roughly 20 to 1 up to 100 to 1. They do, in fact, have some green materials, including grass clippings and home fruit and vegetable wastes. Included in this group would be materials like coffee grounds, straw, and leaves.

Brown compost materials: Brown compost materials fall in the carbon to nitrogen ratio range higher than 100 to 1. This group includes woody materials like saw dust, wood chips, bark, and newspaper. Shredded wood chips or bark are a good options for mixing with grass clippings, as they tend to prevent the grass clippings from settling into a dense mass that will not compost quickly.

For the best decomposition, the organic material should be mixed and added in layers. A layer of soil should be added between the layers — roughly every 8 inches or so. The soil brings along a variety of microorganisms that enhance the decomposition activities. The compost pile should be watered thoroughly and kept moist, but not saturated. As new materials are added, the compost should be re-watered.

There are a few materials not typically included in most compost piles. Meat residues and wastes from the kitchen are not always included because there is some odor associated as they rot and this can attract vermin. Pet and human waste are also not included due to the potential for disease organisms. There is perpetual debate in the gardening community about the wisdom of adding garden waste that might be infected with disease to the compost pile. The general consensus is, in an active compost pile with temperatures reaching 140 to 145 degrees Fahrenheit, all disease-causing bacterial, viral, or fungal organisms will be killed and not pose a threat to the next season crop. However, if you are not confident about your composting process, the safest approach is to discard diseased plant waste in another area away from the vegetable garden.

There are multiple construction options for building your compost pile that depend on the space you have available, the garden space you want to use the compost in, and the aesthetics that you want to achieve. There are multiple vendors selling plastic bins, some that are on stands that rotate easily. Other gardeners choose to build wood, block, stone, or wire enclosures with more aesthetic appeal. Having the sides constructed with openings helps to keep aerobic decomposition active. Many compost bins are constructed with three sides to facilitate accessing the pile for turning or using. The simplest approach is to pile the materials into a heap. This approach probably takes up the most space. While a simple pile of compost may not have the most aesthetic appeal, landscaping around the compost pile can create an effective disguise.

After the compost pile is collected, organisms in the pile will begin to decompose. The first phase of decomposition relies on bacteria in the compost. In this period, bacterial populations and the compost temperature grow rapidly. After much of the carbon in the mix has been decomposed, the bacteria begin to fade. Fungus and protozoans then take over the digestive process. In the final phase, earthworms, centipedes, and other insects continue the process. In warmer months, the temperature of the center of the pile can reach from 110 to 140 degrees Fahrenheit. Temperatures can continue to rise up to 170 to 180 degrees Fahrenheit, but at these temperatures, many beneficial organisms — including the composting organisms — begin to die off. As a result, decomposition slows down, the pile cools down, and organism populations recover. A long-stem thermometer is a handy tool for monitoring decomposition activity in the compost pile and provides guidance for the best time to turn the pile. The compost should be turned every week if it is decomposing and heating rapidly or every month in cooler weather, when the decomposition process is slower. Turning moves the cooler materials to the inside of the pile where they will decompose more readily. Good decomposition requires oxygen, so the other purpose of turning the pile is to aerate the compost. The time it takes for a compost to mature and be ready to add to the garden can be anywhere from three to nine months depending on temperature, moisture, and composition.

The compost pile is an important strategy for the gardener to deliver organic structure to the garden. While the focus of this chapter is growing organic tomatoes, a compost pile can be an important tool for other growers who may not be purists about organic gardening but still need to add organic matter to the soil to provide improved structure and porosity. If high-nitrogen manures are not readily available, the grower may choose to create a compost pile and use synthetic fertilizer as a substitute for manure. A balanced fertilizer (like 10-10-10) should be used at the rate of about 1 cup per 25 square feet of area for each layer in the compost pile. The same suggestions apply about watering and turning the compost pile.

Organic fertilizers

In a garden that has grown legume cover crops and had compost added for several years, it is possible the soil has developed an adequate and sustainable supply of nitrogen and no extra addition of nitrogen is needed. However, these measures will sometimes need to be supplemented with other nitrogen-rich sources to successfully grow tomato plants in newer gardens. There are some materials that qualify as organic and can be added during the growing season to enrich nutrients in the soil. In general, these materials need to be used in larger quantities than what was used for synthetic fertilizers because these contain a smaller percentage of nitrogen. The following are materials to consider supplementing nutrients with when growing tomatoes organically:

Alfalfa Meal: This is commonly used as an animal feed and contains about 3 percent nitrogen that is released in the garden over about one to three months. The advantage of alfalfa meal is that it is usually readily available from animal feed supply stores. The disadvantage is that it can include alfalfa seeds that will contribute to weeds in the garden.

Blood Meal: This is dried, powdered blood and is a byproduct from animal processing facilities. It is relatively expensive, but does provide a ready source of easily accessible nitrogen. Nitrogen is released to be available to the plant in one to four months. The standard analysis is 12-0-0, so it is comparable to synthetic fertilizer in nitrogen content and should be applied in comparable quantities. In addition to nitrogen, blood meal also provides a few micronutrients, including iron.

Wood Ash: Wood ash is not an adequate source of nitrogen, but does provide a good source of phosphorous and potassium. It can also be used to raise the soil pH if the soil is too acidic. Some care should be exercised in adding too much wood ash, as salt content in the soil can become too high.

Fish Emulsion: This organic fertilizer is produced from the by-products of fish-processing facilities. It is supplied in a liquid form and should be diluted in water. It is sometimes recommended to dilute the fish emulsion and spray on plant foliage. Fish emulsion has a mineral analysis of 5-2-2.

Pest/Disease Control Without Chemicals

Disease resistance is the weak link in growing organic vegetables. Over the years, every tomato grower will face the challenge of pests or disease that could limit or even destroy the tomato crop. Fortunately, tomatoes are fairly resilient plants and are probably one of the easier crops to grow organically. Healthy tomato plants resist the influence of a minor disease infection or a small population of insects.

Crop rotation

Crop rotation can be an important strategy to avoid soil-borne diseases in any tomato garden. In organic gardens where chemical pesticides are avoided, crop rotation is even more critical.

Tomatoes and other plants in the same Solanaceae family (egg-plant, peppers, and potatoes) should not be planted in the same area for three years after growing tomatoes in the area. This can be challenging in home gardens where space might be limited, but is important to managing disease without chemicals. In gardens where space is a premium and crop rotation is not an option, using cover crops and compost becomes even more important. Composted manure and legume cover crops will support the growth and activity of beneficial microorganisms in the soil, which will help to combat disease-causing organisms.

Soil solarization

Soil solarization is an interesting organic approach in situations where crop rotation can be impractical. This technique is viable in hot, sunny climates. A clear plastic film is used to cover the soil for four to six weeks during the hottest part of the year. This heats the soil to a temperature that can kill many soil pathogens and weed seeds. In the best conditions, the soil will be heated up to 140 degrees Fahrenheit. A thin piece of polyethylene, usually about 1 mil (0.001 inch) works best. Black plastic — such as is used for mulch — will not heat the soil nearly as effectively as the clear plastic. Experiments also indicate that two layers of thin plastic will drive the heat up more quickly. Separate the layers by an inch or so with spacers. It is also important to till the soil thoroughly and saturate the soil with water immediately before covering. The plastic film should lie as flat as possible on the soil to increase contact, and the edges should be buried in the soil to limit air influx. Plastic films for this purpose can be purchased in home and garden stores or ordered on the Internet. They are often available as painting drop cloths in home improvement stores. Soil solarization is particularly effective against the bacteria that cause bacterial canker, the fungus that causes Fusarium wilt and

Verticillium wilt, and a number of different types of nematodes. You can increase the effectiveness of solarization by adding animal manure — particularly chicken manure — to the soil before tilling, watering, and covering. The heat will cause rapid decomposition of the manure and the generation of ammonia, which is toxic to many microorganisms.

Organic agents to fight pests and disease

In some cases, despite best efforts to provide healthy soil and good growing conditions, insects or disease will threaten your tomato plants. There are a number of materials containing insecticide or disease-fighting properties that qualify as organic and would be appropriate to use in growing organic tomato plants. For the commercial grower, there is a list of agents approved for use in organic farming by the National Organic Program. As would be expected, there is always some debate about the specific materials included in this group. In principle, though, the target is to always use materials extracted from a natural — rather than a synthesized — source and to use materials that do not have a negative impact on the natural flora and fauna in the environment. Following are a few of the organic pesticides sometimes helpful in attempting to grow tomatoes organically:

Pyrethrums: Pyrethrums is a mixture of materials derived from the flower of a particular species of the chrysanthemum plant. It has been used for centuries as a pesticide, with records from the early 1800s of it being used to kill fleas and body lice. It is effective against a wide variety of insect pests and can be used on plants and fruit right up to the time of harvest. Pyrethrum is not particularly stable in sunlight, so is only active about 12 hours after it is applied.

Neem: Neem is extracted from the nut of the neem tree, which is native to Asia but is now grown in a number of tropical climates. The neem extract is sold as an insecticide in two different versions: The most potent chemical extracted from the neem nut is called *azadirachtin* and is marketed under several brand names. The oil part of the extract is sold as Neem Oil and is labeled as a fungicide, insecticide, and miticide. Neem-based products are most effective against aphids and spider mites. Like many organic pesticides, neem is not stable for a long period of time once it is applied so must be reapplied if the target insect persists.

Bacillus Thuringiensis: Bacillus thuringiensis — often abbreviated as Bt — is referred to as a biological insecticide as it is actually a bacterium that creates disease in numerous insects. It is particularly effective against leaf-feeding worms like the tomato hornworm. It is sold under the brand names Dipel® and Thuricide® among others.

Copper Fungicides: Copper fungicides are not explicitly derived from plant or animal sources, but are listed as acceptable for organic gardening. They are typically used as a last resort when other measures have not been effective. Copper fungicides are particularly useful for helping with fungal blight diseases. While they will not cure blight, they will delay plant destruction for three to four weeks if used appropriately. Copper fungicides should not be used too aggressively year after year, as there is some concern for accumulation of copper salts in the soil.

Beneficial Insects: Another strategy sometimes used by organic tomato gardeners for managing insect damage is the deliberate introduction of beneficial predatory insects to your garden. This is only helpful in specific situations and when there is a safe predatory insect available for a high population of a specific pest to your plants. If the pest population is not high enough, the predatory insects will dissipate quickly and find food elsewhere. Examples for tomato pests include ladybugs to control aphids and beneficial nematodes to control a variety of soil-borne organisms.

Best Tomato Varieties to Choose for Organic Growing

One of the most significant things the organic tomato gardener can do is choose disease-resistant varieties of tomatoes. There is an ever-increasing number of hybrid tomatoes on the market today with resistance to a number of bacterial and fungal diseases. There are even some heirloom varieties recommended as disease-resistant against some organisms. It is worth including heirloom varieties in your organic tomato garden for both diversity and variety. Listed are some varieties popular with organic gardeners based on their disease resistance. Several of these are from the Mountain series of tomatoes, developed at North Carolina State University, and are grown by both home and fresh-market growers because they are tasty and have multiple disease resistances.

Mountain Magic: This indeterminate grape tomato cultivar is the newest of the fresh-market cultivars in the Mountain series. It has both early- and late-blight resistance as well as resistance to Verticillium and Fusarium wilt. It has good crack resistance and performed well in taste tests relative to a number of heirloom varieties.

Mountain Supreme: This is a determinate cultivar. It is a medium-sized, deep red hybrid recommended for its resistance to Early Blight. It is also resistant to Verticillium and Fusarium wilt.

Mountain Spring: This is a determinate cultivar that produces large, red fruit. It is resistant to Verticillium and Fusarium wilt (VF) and is resistant to cracking and to blossom end rot.

Mountain Fresh Plus: This is a relatively large, red tomato that is determinate. It has Verticillium and Fusarium wilt resistance and shows tolerance to early blight. It is also resistant to root-knot nematodes.

Mountain Belle: This is a red cherry tomato variety containing the typical Verticillium and Fusarim wilt resistance that is also resistant to cracking and bursting. It is a determinate cultivar that grows well on a relatively short stake.

Muriel Tomato: This is a red, Roma paste tomato targeted for gardens in the Southeast. It is resistant to Verticillium and Fusarium wilt, nematodes, and tomato spotted wilt virus (TSWV).

Legend: This is a hybrid determinate variety that was introduced in 2003. It is known for being one of a small group of tomatoes resistant to late blight. It is a medium-sized red variety that was developed in Oregon and grows well in cool climates.

Chapter 10:
Heirloom Tomatoes

While heirloom tomatoes have, by definition, been around for generations, they have grown enormously popular in the last decade. While the tomato is probably the most popular heirloom vegetable with the most available varieties, there are also heirloom beans, melons, and other popular American vegetables. Additionally, there are heirloom varieties of flowers and herbs. A multitude of dedicated home gardeners have embraced heirloom tomatoes and committed themselves to growing tomatoes, saving seeds, and sharing seeds with other gardeners to preserve for the next generation. There are several wonderful books dedicated to heirloom tomatoes, which have contributed to the growing interest in these tomatoes. There are also multiple Web sites and seed companies dedicated exclusively to heirloom varieties. The heirloom tomato is not an American concept; in fact, many of the most popular heirloom varieties came to the United States via immigrants from around the world who brought along favorite family seeds to add to the farms and gardens in their new homes. The heirloom concept is also very popular in Australia, Europe, and the United Kingdom where they are called heritage varieties.

The love for heirloom tomatoes blends an appetite and taste for tomatoes, a passion for gardening, and an embrace of tradition and history. The interest in heirloom varieties runs parallel to the growth of the local gardening movement, the interest in eating healthy, natural foods, and the enthusiasm for diverse cooking and eating experiences. It also speaks to an increasing discomfort with the American large-scale agricultural industry, and a desire to better understand and participate in the source and supply of the food on our kitchen tables.

Heirloom Definition

Defining the heirloom tomato is not a simple task. It is believed the word was first used in the 1970s. Unlike a hybrid tomato, an heirloom tomato is open-pollinated, meaning that they can be pollinated by flowers on the same plant or by other plants of the same variety or by other tomato plants of different varieties. Hybrid tomato plants are generally self-pollinating, meaning the flower pollinates itself. In fact, the flower anatomy of a hybrid tomato variety includes the male stamen completely surrounding and enveloping the female organ (the pistil) of the flower, so as to preclude open pollination. In the flower of an heirloom tomato, the pistil extends beyond the male stamen; therefore, self-pollination

— while common — is not guaranteed. *For more information on the botanical or scientific definition of heirloom tomatoes, see Chapter 2.*

Some claim that the lower yields of heirloom varieties relative to hybrid varieties is related to the anatomy difference of the flowers. The most significant impact of this difference in hybrid and heirloom tomatoes is that unlike hybrid tomatoes, the seeds of heirloom tomatoes run true. This means that in the absence of mutations or accidental cross-pollination with another tomato varieties, the seeds of the fruit can be saved and replanted the next season to produce identical fruit. As described previously, this is not true with hybrid seeds. Hybrid seeds that are saved and replanted will not uniformly produce fruit like the original plant and, if they are saved for several generations, the seeds will revert back to some having the traits of the mother plant and others having traits of the father plant.

The characterization of heirlooms was clarified somewhat by Carolyn Male in her book devoted to heirloom tomatoes. In her book, she classifies heirloom tomatoes into four different categories: Family Heirlooms, Commercial Heirlooms, Created Heirlooms, or Mystery Heirlooms. This classification helps the home gardener to understand heirlooms better, but there remains some overlap within the groups.

Family Heirlooms: These are the most traditional definition of an heirloom tomato. This is a variety that was selected from the garden for particular traits and from which the seeds were saved and passed down within a family from generation to generation. Most common is the requirement that the variety must have been around for at least 50 years. Others claim the variety must have been grown for at least 100 years. For some of these family heirloom varieties, the lineage of the seed has been re-searched and documented.

Commercial Heirloom: This is the second category of heirloom varieties. This group contains open-pollinated varieties whose original history may have been lost, but were offered for sale by seed companies before the 1940s. Some of these seed companies continue to exist and market seeds. Others failed or were bought up by other larger companies.

Created Heirlooms: This is the third category of heirlooms, and is somewhat of a blend of hybrid and heirlooms. Here, gardeners will deliberately cross two heirlooms plants or an heirloom and a hybrid tomato plant. The resulting seed that is produced has to be grown out for numerous years to isolate the seeds with the traits being sought. This essentially dehybridizes the seeds and creates a variety where the desired traits are realized, but unlike with hybrids, the seeds will run true.

Mystery Heirlooms: This is the final category of heirlooms, and includes new varieties produced from accidental cross-pollina-tion of heirloom tomato plants or from mutations that occur nat-urally. This is essentially the root mechanism that happened in the past and is responsible for the creation of all original heir-loom varieties. These plants were then noticed and selected by careful past growers and saved by generations of growers. The difference here is this accidental crossing or mutation occurs in more recent times and does not have the history that other classi-cal heirlooms have.

Why Grow Heirlooms

Some gardeners have become dedicated to heirloom varieties and find no reason to grow hybrid cultivars. Others choose to include a mix of hybrids and heirlooms in their gardens. Other gardeners try an heirloom variety or two without success and quickly revert to growing a garden of only hybrids. There are several advantages heirlooms have over hybrids that influence a gardener to choose to grow heirloom varieties of tomatoes.

Advantages

Variety: While there are hundreds of hybrid tomato cultivars available for the home gardener, there tends to be a thread of commonality in type among these tomatoes. In the hybrids, you more likely will find round, red varieties with thicker skins and a more predictable traditional tomato taste and consistency. Hybrids are most often developed with the commercial grower in mind. With this, hybrid cultivars tend to favor those traits that support longer shelf life, easier shipping and handling, and more uniform sizes and shapes. Some of the traits that make homegrown tomatoes most appealing — thin skins and juicy textures — are deliberately bred out in hybrids. The heirlooms, on the other hand, offer an array of colors, sizes, shapes, textures, and taste. Some even stretch the classic expectation of what tomatoes should look and taste like. Many local food restaurants have a particular fondness for specific heirloom tomato varieties because the varying colors, shapes, and tastes make for creative salad recipes. There are also more heirloom varieties available to the home gardener than there are hybrids. There are roughly 600 different heirloom varieties available from various seed sources and exchanges.

Seed saving: As explained, one of the key factors distinguishing heirloom tomato varieties from hybrids is that the heirloom seeds run true. This means that — unlike hybrids — if you grow an heirloom tomato, you are able to collect some of the seeds during harvest and save them for the next year's garden. This offers you an economical advantage because you have a free source of tomato seeds for the next season's garden. It also offers a practical advantage of a sure supply of seeds for yourself or for your gardening friends. It is not unusual for seed companies to update their collection of seeds and discontinue varieties that might not be as popular as others.

Heritage and diversity: There is also a philosophical or ideological reason for growing heirloom tomatoes: because it brings the past alive and reinforces an appreciation of gardening heritage. It also contributes to maintaining broad genetic diversity in the human agricultural portfolio, which will help to maintain the health and sustainability of our food supply. A diverse genetic portfolio of tomato varieties will ensure that people maintain varieties that are healthy and resilient to a variety of environmental challenges. Limiting the gene pool by growing only hybrid varieties will ultimately make the plants more susceptible to pests and disease.

Disadvantages

It is difficult to characterize the problems you might run into when growing heirlooms; this is because there is a large variety of heirlooms with a broad array of characteristics. As an example, while the average hybrid may have a longer shelf life than the average heirloom, it is certainly possible to find specific varieties of heirlooms that have an extended shelf life. Consequently, the disadvantages described here are meant to reflect the general characteristics of hybrids versus heirlooms and not meant to imply that all heirlooms have a particular disadvantage.

The subject of heirlooms and disease resistance deserves some discussion. There is debate in the gardening community about the disease resistance of hybrids versus heirlooms. It is true that there are a number of hybrid tomato varieties that have been deliberately bred to achieve a high degree of resistance to specific tomato diseases. Good experimental data exists to support the disease resistance of many of these varieties. Conversely, it can also be argued that some heirloom varieties have had hundreds of years to evolve a resistance to various pests and diseases. Over the centuries, various varieties have adapted to grow well in particular climates and geographies and to survive exposure to many of the challenges that might be presented in these areas. There was one study in Maryland that found that two heirloom varieties — Pink Brandywine and Ukranian Olena — were more resistant than two hybrid varieties. The heirloom varieties were both of the potato-leaf type, and one theory is that the potato leaf is thicker and more resistant to foliage disease. In order to realize the benefits of growing heirlooms in general, you may have to do some research and grow a number of different heirloom varieties to find those best suited to flourish in your particular climate and against your particular disease-causing pathogens. If you have had significant issues with particular tomato diseases in past years, be sure to pick varieties that promise some resistance to that disease. This, of course, applies to whether you are growing heirlooms or hybrids.

Disease resistance: While the question of heirlooms being less disease resistance than hybrids is arguable, it is certainly true that it is more difficult to ascertain which heirlooms should be resistant to which tomato diseases. There have been many more studies done with hybrids and this — in combination with the breeding process — has allowed the development of a simple naming system that spells out disease resistance pretty clearly for hybrids. More research is required on the gardener's part to explore the experience of others in your area with heirlooms and their resistance to particular diseases.

Storage: In general, hybrid tomatoes have a better shelf life than heirloom varieties. This is most often a factor for commercial growers, but may also be a factor in your garden if you want to have more flexibility in using and storing your harvest.

Training: The overwhelming majority of heirloom tomato plants are indeterminate. They tend to grow prolific vines that can be difficult to train and control. This can be a problem, especially if you are trying to grow tomatoes in a small area or in containers on a deck or patio.

Growing Tips for Heirlooms

In general, the same principles apply for growing heirloom tomatoes as for growing hybrid tomatoes. In practice, successfully growing heirlooms boils down to emphasizing some general recommended practices more than others:

- Sow an ample number of seeds when growing heirlooms. In general, you are more likely to find heirloom varieties that have lower germination rates than hybrids.

- Experiment with a number of different varieties to find the ones that have the most vigor in your specific area. This may be varieties suited to your climate or may be varieties that have evolved with some resistance to diseases common in your area.

- Leverage disease-avoidance techniques more aggressively, including crop rotation, mulching, and drip irrigation.

- Give heirloom tomato plants a little extra space to grow. The vigorous long vines that are typical of heirloom plants will produce more if given space to spread. In addition, the extra breathing space between plants will help to mitigate the development and spread of some tomato diseases.

Saving Heirloom Seeds

Tomato seeds are fairly easy to save for germination in later seasons. The typical home gardener has probably had occasions where "volunteer" tomato plants appeared in the garden or the compost area. This is a result of tomatoes that were left on the ground and had seeds that settled into the soil and naturally over-wintered to be ready to sprout the next spring. Saving seeds is simply a deliberate and more-controlled version of this.

Seeds should be collected from several fruits from a plant. Choose the healthiest and most vigorous plants and fruits you can. Pick the fruit after it has fully colored, but before it has a chance to over-ripen. The tomato contains a gelatinous material around the seeds, which serves the purpose of inhibiting germination while the seed is in the fruit. The seeds should be fermented to both break down the gelatinous inhibitor and to destroy any pathogens that might be present. Fermentation will occur naturally if the juice and seeds are placed in a small container, covered, and allowed to sit for two to three days. The seeds will normally sink to the bottom and the pulp and gel will float on the surface. After two to three days, strain the seeds from the juice. You may need to add water to help separate the seeds from the gelatinous material. Spread the seeds on a paper plate or towel and allow them to dry naturally at room temperature. After drying, store the seeds in the refrigerator or the freezer. Multiple packets can be carefully labeled and stored in a single moisture-proof glass or plastic container. A drying agent — such as powdered milk or silica gel — can be added to the container to help keep the seeds dry. Seeds stored this way should be viable for at least five years. Be sure and label seeds carefully as all tomato seeds look basically alike.

Seed Sources for Heirlooms

There are a number of different sources for finding heirloom varieties for your garden. There are two organizations that are non-profit and have a mission dedicated to collecting heirloom seeds of vegetables, flowers, and herbs. *For more information on sources for finding heirloom varieties, see Appendix A.*

1. **Southern Seed Savers Exchange:** This company was started in 1982 and is based in Monticello, Virginia. While they emphasize varieties adapted to the mid-Atlantic and the South, they have seeds that are appropriate for all of the United States and Canada. They are a source for heirloom seeds for a wide variety of vegetables, herbs, flowers, grains, and fruits and have a large selection of heirloom tomato seeds. They also have a large focus on growing organic seeds. Southern Seed Savers Exchange is focused on collecting, preserving, and distributing heirloom seeds as well as developing new high-performance, open-pollinated varieties with desirable traits. They

grow some of their own seeds and also rely on a network of growers that support their enterprise.

2. **The Seed Savers Exchange:** Seed Savers Exchange has more than 10,000 members and a mission of saving the world's diverse but endangered garden heritage for future generations. It is essentially a network of people committed to collecting, conserving, and sharing heirloom seeds and plants. Seed Savers Exchange began in 1975 when two seeds — Grandpa Ott's Morning Glory and German Pink Tomato — were brought from Bavaria to the United States in the late 1800s and were later passed down to Seed Savers cofounders. Seed Savers maintains thousands of heirloom vegetables, herbs, and flowers and has more than 5,000 varieties of tomatoes in its collection.

Popular Heirloom Tomatoes

As there are thousands of heirloom varieties that have been grown and hundreds of heirloom tomatoes currently available commercially to the home gardener, choosing the best for your garden and listing them here would be impossible. The other problem is that 'best' is clearly in the eyes of the beholder and also strongly influenced by your specific gardening environment. While your choice of which type to grow should certainly not be limited to these listed here, the following are a few of the most popular and most interesting heirloom varieties:

Mortgage Lifter: This is a popular variety for both its taste and for its story. The Mortgage Lifter is an example of a Created Heirloom. A West Virginia radiator repairman, M.C. "Radiator Charlie" Byles, created it in the 1930s. Byles had no formal plant-breeding experience. He mixed pollen from four different tomato varieties with extra large fruit and after seven years of planting and collecting seeds, came up with a stable variety. Byles then grew and sold the seedlings. He eventually made enough money selling these plants that he was able to pay off the mortgage on his home. The tomato was then forever known as the Mortgage Lifter. The Mortgage Lifter tomato is a large, pinkish-red fruit that ranges from 1 to 3 pounds. It has a meaty texture with few seeds and is good for slicing.

Abe Lincoln: This is an example of a commercial heirloom. It was introduced in 1923 by the W. H. Buckbee Seed Company of Illinois and named for the president who called the state home. It is a late-maturing variety and produces classic, medium-sized red fruit (roughly 8 to 16 ounces). It was introduced back before seed companies shifted to hybrid tomatoes. This type survived largely because it was a classic, solid producer.

Brandywine: This is a large pink tomato of the potato-leaf type. The potato leaf does not have the more-typical serrated edges of most tomato plants. Brandywine is a large, pink variety with fruits weighing up to 2 pounds and is one of the most popular heirloom varieties offered by Seed Savers Exchange. Brandywine tomatoes have a cloudy history. They were listed in the late 1800s in both a Johnson & Stokes and a Burpee seed catalogue. In the early 1900s, the variety disappeared from all commercial seed catalogs. It turned up again in 1982 as a donation to the Seed Savers Exchange, and had apparently been handed down in a family through several generations. Brandywine is also a good illustration of the inconsistency found from time to time with heirloom varieties. There are multiple versions of the Brandywine tomato offered by different seed companies, oftentimes producing very different fruits. There are also many other heirlooms with versions of the name — including Yellow Brandywine, Black Brandywine, and Plum Brandywine — some of which are probably related to the original Brandywine variety.

Chocolate Stripes: This tomato is one of those easily identified as an heirloom from its unusual shape and deep mahogany color laced with green stripes. It has a sweet, smoky taste. Like many heirloom varieties, it grows on a large indeterminate vine. It is very tolerant to cool weather and will continue producing well into the fall.

German Red Strawberry: This is a variety with a German heritage classified as a family heirloom. It has a shape that is reminiscent of a super-large red strawberry. In the right environment, the German Red Strawberry can be a high-volume producer, with yields generally much higher than most heart-shaped tomatoes. The individual fruit can weigh up to 1 pound. This variety is also popular because of its sweet flavor.

Plum Lemon: This is another tomato clearly distinguishable as an heirloom based on its unusual shape and color. The fruit are bright yellow and even have a slight point on the bottom end that liken them even more to a lemon. The Plum Lemon has the size of the typical plum tomato (about 5 ounces). The yellow color runs through the skin and meat, so it makes for colorful salads. These seeds were sourced from Russia.

Kellogg's Breakfast: This is a giant beefsteak variety that grows to a bright orange color both inside and out. The fruit routinely pass the 1-pound mark and some weigh in up to 2 pounds. Apparently, it was first cultivated by a Michigan gardener named Kellogg and would be classified as a family heirloom. It is meaty and juicy, and it makes for flavorful and tasty tomato sandwiches. It is popular both for its excellent taste and its reputation for being hardy and resistant to various tomato maladies.

Mr. Stripey: Mr. Stripey is an heirloom variety that is a member of the created heirloom group. It was originally selected and stabilized in England and was known as Tigerella. It is bicolored; generally characterized as red with yellow stripes. The plant is particularly striking when the fruits are at different ripening stages with a diversity of color combinations. The fruit is the size of a large plum, about 6 ounces.

Cherokee Purple: This heirloom is reported to be more than 100 years old. The Cherokee Indians are credited as originally growing the variety. This historical tidbit has caught the fascination of a number of heirloom growers and probably somewhat accounts for its popularity. It is recognized for its dusky purple color and green shoulders. They are a beefsteak-style variety with large plants and large fruit. It is reported to be a good tomato to grow in the south with some level of disease resistance.

Chapter 11:

Harvesting and Using Your Tomato Crop

Harvesting

Timing

For home use and for canning, tomatoes should ideally be picked when fully ripened: When they are fully colored and firm. When collecting in baskets, removing the stems is important to prevent the stem from puncturing other tomatoes. When tomatoes are ripe they bruise easily, so be careful about dropping them into baskets or containers. In some situations where birds, squirrels, or other pests are prevalent, collecting tomatoes before fully ripe may allow you to harvest more undamaged fruit. Also, extremely hot temperatures (in the mid- to high- 90s) can prevent fruit from ripening and coloring well. In this situation, you should pick when the fruit is partially ripe and allow them to ripen indoors. Animals will often only snack on tomatoes that are fully ripened. Semi-ripened fruits will ripen nicely on kitchen countertops or in the pantry. Never refrigerate tomatoes that are not yet ripe because it prevents them from ripening further. For those recipes that call for unripe green tomatoes, it is best to wait until the fruits are full size, but have not yet begun to turn red. The small green tomatoes that have not yet grown to full size will have a somewhat bitter taste.

Extending the tomato season

In some locations, tomato plants may still be loaded with fruit as the first fall frost approaches. If the plant foliage is still healthy, consider some protection for your plants. Mature tomato plants can survive freezing temperatures into the upper 20s, which can sometimes occur without any visible frost. On the other hand, frost can kill plants and can occur on plant surfaces, in low-lying areas, when air temperatures are above freezing. The frosts come in two different varieties. In some cases, a cold front moves into the area and temperatures may drop precipitously. In this situation, attempts at protection may be futile. The other frost situation is when you still are having warm days, but a calm and clear night allows heat from the earth to escape leading to a frost. In this situation, you have a good chance of extending your plant's production for potentially several more weeks.

If you are container gardening, you have an obvious advantage in your effort to protect against the fall frost. This is also where pots on wheels offer a convenient opportunity for moving plants. For minor frosts, just moving plants under an awning or porch covering can provide enough protection. For heavier frosts, moving into a garage or basement might be in order.

For garden plants, covering is the first line of defense. This approach relies on trapping heat from the soil and preventing it from escaping the area around your plants. Apply the covers an hour or so before the sun goes down to catch the heat before the soil warms. Cover plants with burlap, old sheets, tarps or heavy paper. Plastic sheets can also be used as covers, although some wire frames are a good idea to avoid contact of the plastic with the tomato plants. If you have only a few tomato plants, putting some small lights under the covering, to add a little extra heat, is reasonable. To allow the sun to re-warm the soil, the covering must be removed during the day. While the exact amount of protection you will get depends on specific local conditions, including humidity and wind, it is not unreasonable to expect tomato plants to survive up to four degrees below freezing with coverings alone.

 **Tomato Tidbits**

Emergency metallic blankets can help your tomatoes by warming the garden. This is an interesting use for the blankets, which are often available at camping supply stores. These blankets have an aluminum layer on one side and are sometimes called space blankets. Place the metallic side toward the soil to reflect heat back to the tomato plants. In garden trials in Colorado, gardeners using a combination of Christmas lights and a metallic blanket were able the raise the temperature under the blanket by more than 20 degrees.

Water can also be used as a protection against freezing temperatures. Water sprinklers should be turned on the tomato plants before the temperature drops below freezing and not be turned off until it rises again above freezing. To manage this in the fall, sprinklers can be put on timers and set to turn on just before dawn when temperatures are the lowest.

If the temperature looks like it is dropping too much and for too long a period of time to manage, pick and bring inside unripe tomatoes for ripening. All-green tomatoes will not ripen off the vine. Green tomatoes must have reached a mature stage on the plant before they can be picked and expected to ripen indoors. If your tomatoes have a pinkish tinge of color, you can certainly expect them to ripen easily indoors. If you have numerous green tomatoes, you can sacrifice one of them to confirm that they are mature enough for ripening. A mature green tomato will either have a yellow tinged fruit or have developed a gel-like pulp in the interior. If the sacrificed tomato is ripe, most tomatoes of a similar size will also be sufficiently mature to ripen well. For smaller green tomatoes that will not ripen, use them in recipes that call for green tomatoes.

Sunlight is not needed to ripen tomatoes. The best approach is to spread them in a single layer in a box or tray with a layer of newspaper strips between each row of tomatoes. The newspaper will prevent the tomatoes from touching and inhibit the possible spread of any disease. Another storage option is to place the tomatoes in trays spread with Styrofoam storage peanuts to assure air circulation around the fruit. If you have an ample collection of green tomatoes for ripening, group any tomatoes that are just beginning to show signs of color separately, so that you do not have to search for them later. Tomatoes should be placed in a dark pantry or basement where the temperature is between 55 and 70 degrees Fahrenheit. The tomatoes will typically ripen over a period of three to four weeks. Check the tomatoes carefully each day or so for any sign of disease or decay and remove any individual fruits that show such signs. If you would like to have some of the tomatoes ripen more quickly than others, take a few of the tomatoes out and place in a paper bag with the top folded over to close. Tomatoes naturally produce ethylene gas, which helps to stimulate ripening. Enclosing the tomatoes in the paper sack will contain some of the ethylene gas and speed up the ripening process. Another interesting trick is to place a partially green banana in the bag with the green tomatoes to increase the amount of ethylene and boost ripening.

Preparing the Site for Next Season

The last job of the garden season is not harvesting; it is taking advantage of the mild fall weather to prepare the garden for the next season. This preparation will help to maximize the texture, organic content, and moisture-holding capability of the soil for your next garden. Remove any diseased plants from the garden. If possible, do not place diseased plants in your compost or leave them close to the garden to decay. Fall is the best time to add lime to the garden. Check your soil for pH and adjust per package instructions. Cover your garden soil with 4 to 6 inches of organic mulch. If you plant a winter cover crop, till in the organic matter and plant your cover crop. If not, allow compost to stay on the soil over the winter to control erosion and weed growth.

Cooking With Tomatoes

The fact that tomatoes are so popular in the home garden is directly related the versatility of the tomato in the kitchen. Tomatoes are the central ingredient in a variety of recipes, including appetizers, soups, salads, beverages, condiments, main courses, and even desserts. Tomatoes can be used fresh from the garden and raw, and can be cooked into savory sauces and stews. While conventional wisdom says that eating vegetables raw is healthier, some of the health benefits of tomatoes actually improve when they are cooked. Food scientists have found that, while the content of Vitamin C in tomatoes decreases when cooked, the amount of lycopene and other antioxidants in tomatoes actually increases.

Tomatoes can be eaten peeled or unpeeled. The concentration of lycopene is higher in the peel of the tomato than in the meat of the fruit, so you might consider leaving the peel on for some salad and sliced recipes. Health factors aside, many cooks choose to peel tomatoes for many recipes. For sliced tomato recipes, the most appealing way to peel the tomato is the old-fashioned way — with a sharp, flat-edged knife. For these recipes, the tomatoes should be fully ripe, based on the color, but still firm to the touch. In situations where you are using more than one or two tomatoes — and especially when you are planning to cook the tomatoes — they can be peeled easily by dropping them whole into a pot of boiling water for 30 to 60 seconds. Before dropping them in whole, some cooks recommend using a sharp knife to score an "X" through the peel on the bottom end of the tomato, which will aid in peel removal after they are removed from the water. The boiling water causes the water just under the skin to heat and expand, and this pops the skin loose. The tomatoes should be rinsed quickly in cold water to keep the meat from getting hot. Then, the skins can be easily removed.

 Tomato Tidbits

Companies that commercially process tomatoes peel them by flashing with steam or spraying/washing with a concentrated lye solution. The peels are then gently and mechanically scrubbed off the tomatoes.

There are a few common-sense tips to remember when using fresh tomatoes:

- Avoid refrigerating ripe tomatoes. Refrigeration of ripe tomatoes for a few hours can be used to put a nice chill on them before serving; however, never keep tomatoes in the refrigerator for more than a day. When tomatoes are kept below 50 degrees Fahrenheit, the texture of the tomato will begin to soften and become mealy.

- When slicing tomatoes, always do so just before serving, as some of the flavor compounds in tomatoes are volatile and will begin to dissipate if they sit for too long.

- It is much easier to slice tomatoes with a serrated knife than a flat-edge knife. If you use a flat-edge knife and it is not very sharp, you have a good chance of bruising or squashing the tomato.

The diversity and number of recipes for tomatoes is overwhelming, so this is not a comprehensive list of recipes for tomatoes. Included here are classic recipes for dishes that rely on tomatoes as one of the primary ingredients.

Favorite ripe tomato recipes

Most often, tomatoes are used fully ripened and are used raw as often as they are used cooked. Raw tomatoes are generally incorporated into salads, soups, and side dishes. Cooked tomatoes are found in stews, soups, and baked dishes. They are often found in dishes of Italian, Spanish, or Mexican origin.

Insalata Caprese

This is a very simple Italian salad that makes basic sliced tomatoes look and taste special. One can use either standard slicing tomatoes or any plum tomatoes to make this dish. While the standard recipe is tomatoes, basil leaves, and mozzarella cheese, you can make variations by adding finely chopped garlic, fresh parsley, chopped black olives, or capers. While the traditional dressing for Insalata Caprese is olive oil, you can use other types of dressings. With sweet, ripe, red tomatoes, flavored vinegars are great dressings for this salad. Balsamic vinegar is often used. In the summer, it helps to keep a small spray bottle with balsamic vinegar handy to make "drizzling" easier. Purists like to use fresh mozzarella cheese made from water buffalo milk, which can be found in many gourmet cheese stores.

Ingredients:

Sliced tomatoes

Fresh mozzarella cheese, sliced

Fresh basil leaves

Salt and pepper

Olive oil

Alternate tomatoes and mozzarella cheese slices staggered in a circle around a plate. Place fresh basil leaves on top of the slices. Season with salt and pepper. Drizzle with olive oil.

Gazpacho

Gazpacho is a chilled vegetable soup with tomatoes as the primary ingredient. It is primarily identified as a Spanish dish, but is also popular in many parts of South America. As always, there are many variations to the recipe. Some expand the list of vegetables below to include chopped sweet peppers or avocados. Some choose to puree the vegetables in a food processor. Others prefer the visual and taste appeal of finely chopped vegetables. Garnish options include cilantro, parsley, bread crumbs and/or a dollop of sour cream.

Ingredients:

2 to 3 lbs tomatoes, peeled

2 crushed garlic cloves

1 onion, chopped

1 to 2 ribs of celery, finely chopped

1 cucumber, finely chopped

2 Tbsp apple cider or red wine vinegar

Salt and pepper to taste

Cilantro

Chop tomatoes, onion, celery, cucumbers, and garlic finely. Combine all ingredients except cilantro and mix well. Salt and pepper to taste. Gazpacho should be made ahead and given two to three hours to chill before serving. Garnish with chopped cilantro.

Pico de Gallo

Pico de Gallo is a chunky, fresh version of salsa. Salsa can be traced back to the Incas, Mayans, and the Aztecs of Mexico and was adopted by the Spanish during the invasion of the 1500s. It was used mostly as a condiment for meat dishes. In the United States, it is a staple of Mexican restaurants and sports bars. Like gazpacho, it is a good reason for the home gardener to add a few extra veggies such as peppers and cucumbers to the backyard garden. Pico de Gallo and salsa can be used as a dip for tortilla chips, a topping for tacos, quesadillas or enchiladas, or as a condiment for chicken or fish.

Ingredients:

3 to 4 medium-size tomatoes, peeled and seeds removed

1 onion

2 jalapeño peppers, seeds removed

1 tbsp lime juice

½ cup fresh cilantro leaves, chopped

1 small clove crushed garlic

Salt and pepper to taste

Chop all ingredients finely and combine together. Chill before serving. If the mix is too juicy, use a sieve to drain off the excess water. This can be prepared in bulk and frozen in small plastic bags for use during the winter. It will not have quite the taste and texture of the garden-fresh version, but it will still be tastier and more fresh than the grocery store option.

Bruschetta

Bruschetta originated in Italy and is most often used as an appetizer. You can think of it as Pico de Gallo on toast. The recipe described here is a basic but delicious version. As usual, there are many variations. They include adding chopped olives, capers, or sweet peppers. As an alternative to browning in olive oil, the bread can be toasted or browned in a skillet.

Ingredients:

2 tomatoes, peeled

½ onion

Chopped fresh basil to taste

1 garlic clove, crushed

Salt and pepper to taste

Olive oil

Italian bread

Chop and mix the tomatoes, onion, garlic, and basil. Add salt and pepper to taste. Allow this to sit while you get the bread ready. Cut the fresh bread into slices and brown in a skillet with the heated olive oil. Try heating the mix in the microwave just to get it warm (about 30 seconds) before putting it on the pan-fried bread slices. If it is too watery, drop the mix into a fine sieve before adding to the bread. Add the tomato mix to the bread. Freshly grated Parmesan cheese can be added to the top if desired.

Aunt V's Tomato Soup

Thanks to Andy Warhol, tomato soup in a can is classic. It is easy to make from scratch and, when served with bread, makes a tasteful and simple dinner or lunch. This basic recipe can be jazzed up by adding crab meat or small shrimp.

Ingredients

4 cups chopped fresh tomatoes

1 chopped onion

2 cups chicken or vegetable broth

½ stick butter

¼ cup flour

¼ cup heavy cream

Salt, pepper, and sugar to taste

In a stock pot, combine onions, tomatoes and broth and bring to a gentle boil for about 20 minutes. In a small pan, melt the butter.

Add flour and make a roux, cooking and stirring until brown and smooth. Add the roux to the tomato and broth mixture. Blend with whisk or hand mixer on low. Add 1/4 cup cream and stir until combined. Season with salt, pepper, and a small amount of sugar. Cook for an additional five minutes.

Baked Eggplant and Tomatoes

In addition to parmigiana and vegetarian lasagna, this recipe and its variations are a good reason to add an eggplant plant to your tomato garden. This makes a good vegetable side dish when serving fish, chicken or beef.

Ingredients:

2 large tomatoes, peeled

1 small eggplant, peeled

Goat cheese

Chopped parsley

Thyme

Olive oil

Preheat oven to 425 degrees Fahrenheit. Slice tomatoes and eggplant into similar-sized rounds about 1/3 inch thick. Dip both into olive oil and arrange in overlapping slices of the eggplant and tomato in a circle in a round baking dish. Season with salt and pepper and garnish with thyme sprigs and parsley. Cover with foil and bake in the oven for 20 minutes. Remove the foil and cook for an additional 25 minutes or until the eggplant is tender. Crumble the goat cheese over the top and bake for an additional ten minutes or until lightly brown. Serve warm. This dish can also be prepared in a grill while cooking a rotisserie chicken or other main dish.

Stuffed Tomatoes

Just like peppers, some of the meaty tomatoes can make a great stuffed dish. As described in Chapter 2, there are some tomato cultivars that are great options for stuffed tomato dishes. The top of the tomato should be sliced off and the pulp and seeds removed. This will leave the ¼ to ½ inch pericarp layer that is attached to the skin. Following are three options for stuffing. The crawfish and sausage make a great main dish and the vegetarian option can be served as a main course or as a side dish. These recipes are based on stuffing four large tomatoes.

Ingredients:

Crawfish Stuffing

⅔ cup rice

1 clove garlic, crushed

1 cup chopped onion

6 Tbsp olive oil

2 Tbsp chopped basil

½ lb crawfish tails

1 cup grated Parmesan

Salt and pepper

Sausage Stuffing

⅔ cup rice

1 clove garlic, crushed

1 cup chopped onion

6 Tbsp olive oil

Several thyme sprigs

½ lb sausage

1 cup shredded Provolone

Salt and pepper

Vegetable Stuffing

$2/3$ cup rice

1 clove garlic, crushed

1 cup chopped onion

6 Tbsp olive oil

2 Tbsp basil

10 oz chopped spinach

½ cup grated Parmesan

Salt and pepper

Instructions for Crawfish, Sausage, and Vegetable Stuffing:

Cook the rice until just barely tender. Cover the bottom of a baking pan with 3 tablespoons of the olive oil. Place the hollowed tomatoes in the pan. In 3 tablespoons of olive oil, sauté the stuffing components and add cheese and spices. Combine the sautéed vegetables or meats with the rice and fill the tomato pots. Sprinkle with a little extra Parmesan cheese. Bake at 350 degrees Fahrenheit for 20 to 25 minutes.

Favorite green tomato recipes

Green tomatoes are valued in recipes both for their firm texture and tangy taste.

These recipes are good for leveraging those benefits as well as for taking advantage of unripe tomatoes salvaged before the first fall frost.

Fried Green Tomatoes

This dish is a Southern classic and somewhat popularized more broadly by the movie of the same name. They are good as an appetizer or as a side dish. They can be served with a variety of sauces, including simple ketchup, a mustard-based sauce, or a sour cream and dill sauce. The batters used for fried green tomatoes range from all flour to all cornmeal based. The one here is a combination of the two. Tomatoes for this recipe should be picked when they reach full size, but before they begin to turn color. Ripe tomatoes can also be fried but they should be picked barely ripe so they are still very firm. Green tomatoes are better for this recipe, as they offer more of a tangy taste.

Ingredients

2 medium to large green tomatoes

Vegetable oil for frying

½ cup flour

¼ cup corn meal

½ tsp salt

1 tsp lemon pepper salt

2 eggs

1 tsp Worcestershire sauce

¼ cup milk

Slice tomatoes about 1/4 inch thick. The thinner that they are sliced, the crispier the final product will be. Combine the flour, corn meal, and seasonings. Whisk the eggs, Worcestershire sauce, and milk together. Dredge the tomato slices in the flour mix, the egg mix, and then the flour mix again. Tomatoes can be fried in a shallow or deep pan. The oil should be hot enough so the tomatoes bubble aggressively when dropped in. Use tongs to turn them over when they begin to brown on the bottom side. Drain thoroughly to remove as much oil as possible and arrange on a paper towel. Serve immediately or keep in a warm oven until ready to serve. Serves four.

Green Tomato Salsa

Salsa with green tomatoes is a great alternative to the Mexican red tomato favorite. As with the red tomato version, there are multiple variations on the green tomato salsa theme. This version includes sweet red peppers to add the familiar red and uses cilantro for flavor. This recipe is cooked rather than fresh and can be eaten immediately after cooking or processed in jars and stored for later use in the winter.

Ingredients

3 lbs. green tomatoes, seeds removed

2 large onions

2 green peppers, seeds removed

1 sweet red pepper, seeds removed

1 to 3 jalapeño peppers depending on taste

2 garlic cloves, crushed

$1/3$ cup fresh cilantro

1 Tbsp parsley

2 ½ Tbsp salt

1 ½ tsp ground black pepper

$2/3$ cup vinegar

$1/3$ cup lemon juice

Finely chop tomatoes, onions, and peppers. Combine everything in a pan and bring to a boil. Let simmer for 15 minutes. Let cool, chill, and serve with tortilla chips. To store for the winter, pour into jars, seal, and process in boiling water for 10 to 15 minutes.

Preserving Tomatoes for Winter

Whether a result of a strained economy or related to the growing enthusiasm for local food, canning and preserving food for the winter is a booming activity. Sales of jars, pressure canners, and other canning supplies are growing; indicative of the growing interest by home gardeners and local market shoppers in preserving the best of the season's abundance.

One of the reasons tomatoes have been a standard for the home gardener for generations is the ability to preserve tomatoes from the garden to last through a long, cold winter. A pantry stocked with carefully labeled jars full of tomatoes always feels like money in the bank. And the variety of recipes tomatoes participate in ensure that these preserved vegetables never go to waste. Tomatoes chosen for preserving should be disease and insect free and washed well. The natural acidity of tomatoes makes them an excellent candidate for preserving, as the acidity will limit the microbial growth. The best and most acidic tomatoes for preserving are always those that have just ripened. Green tomatoes have the most acidity, and as the fruit ripens the acidity drops. Overly ripe fruit and fruit that has been left on a dead or frozen vine will especially tend to be less acidic. Furthermore, just ripened fruit will have the least risk of disease or microbial contamination.

Canning

Canning is the classic and traditional way of preserving tomatoes and other vegetables for use in the winter. Canning, of course, is the misnomer for preserving vegetables and fruits in glass jars. It likely originates from the community canning facilities where, in the past, farmers and home gardeners brought their produce for canning. While these facilities have pretty much disappeared, the home practice of canning is flourishing.

The two basic processes for canning tomatoes are boiling-water canning and pressure canning. Preserving most vegetables and all meats is limited to pressure canning to ensure biological safety, but the acidity of tomatoes makes them a candidate for either type of preservation. Some recommend boiling-water canning as the best approach for tomatoes. This is largely because the equipment is simpler and the time to preserve is less for the boiling-water approach. While the pressure canner allows for a quicker processing time than boiling water, the preparation and cooling time makes the pressure canner process more time intensive. However, others argue that the quality and nutrient value of tomatoes is better from a pressure canner because of the shorter high temperature processing time.

While tomatoes are acidic by nature, the exact pH can vary depending on many factors, including variety of tomatoes, ripeness of tomatoes, and local climate. In the best situation, tomatoes are just acidic enough to be acceptable for boiling water canning. For this reason, the careful gardener will always add acid to ensure the pH is low enough to prevent microbial decomposition from occurring. The pH can be lowered with real or bottled lemon juice, citric acid, or vinegar. Vinegar is usually not recommended, as it has the most impact on the taste of the tomatoes. Citric acid has the least impact on the flavor but bottled lemon juice tends to be the most economical and simplest choice. While, in principle, the canning process has not changed meaningfully over the last 50 years, the National Center for Home Food Preservation has published revised guidelines for an extensive list of foods, including tomatoes, to ensure that food is preserved safely.

Freezing

Freezing tomatoes is an easy and reliable way to preserve them for winter use. Tomatoes preserved this way do lose some of their original texture, but the process is quick and easy and the risk of bacterial contamination is limited. Frozen tomatoes can be used throughout the winter for soups, stews, and sauces. If the tomatoes are disease-free, they can be washed and frozen whole. When thawed, the peels come off easily. Tomatoes can be peeled, halved, or quartered and placed in rigid plastic freezer containers or in plastic freezer bags. Tomatoes can be sieved to remove some of the excess moisture. This is desirable if freezer space is at a premium. The standard recommendation is to eat frozen tomatoes within eight months, although they will generally last for several years. Tomatoes can also be blanched, which is the process of boiling for five to ten minutes to limit bacterial growth and color degradation and to reduce the risk of spoilage, but this is usually not necessary.

Drying

Dried or dehydrated tomatoes can be a nice snack, a topping for salads, a complement to pastas, or a topping for garlic bread or pizzas. The best varieties of tomatoes to dry are generally sauce tomatoes such as Romas that start with a higher solid content. Dried tomatoes can be fairly expensive to buy, but are fairly easy to dry. Drying removes most of the moisture from the tomato so that bacteria, mold, and enzyme activity is inhibited. To dry properly, tomatoes must be dried slowly, so the outside does not crust over and prevent the inside from drying adequately. Wire or plastic mesh screens can be used to support tomatoes to encourage airflow and uniform drying and prevent the need for turning. While sun drying may be the classic method of drying tomatoes, drying in the sun is not generally a practical option in most climates and where the climate might be appropriate, the process can take three to four days and requires consistent hot, low-humidity days with some breeze.

Drying in an oven, while not as romantic as drying in the sun, does offer more consistency and reliability. The best tomatoes for drying tend to be sauce tomatoes because they have more meat and less pulp and gel. Peel tomatoes and slice them into halves or quarter-inch slices. If using large tomatoes, cut them into quarters. Scoop out, discard the seeds, and squeeze any excess juice out of the tomatoes. Spread the tomatoes in shallow pan covered with aluminum foil. Season the tomatoes with salt, pepper, and the dried seasonings of your choice — thyme, oregano, or basil. Place the tomatoes in the oven at 140 degrees Fahrenheit with the oven door slightly ajar to allow moist air to escape. It will take between eight and 16 hours to dry the tomatoes depending on your oven and the type and size of tomato pieces.

You can also use dedicated food dehydrators. These are essentially low-temperature ovens with fans to increase airflow around the food and speed up the drying process. A dehydrator will dry food about twice as fast as an oven and is more energy-efficient. After removing the dried tomatoes from the oven or the dehydrator, they should be allowed to cool to room temperature and then stored in plastic bags, plastic containers, or glass jars — the key requirement is the containers are moisture proof. When stored in a cool, dry location, they should last for six months. Dried tomatoes can also be stored in the freezer or refrigerator. Dried tomatoes can also be packed in glass jars and stored in olive oil, but should then be refrigerated.

Pickling

Pickling tomatoes is another great option for preserving some of your garden produce for the winter. Pickling is very analogous to canning, and some of the same concerns about safety to prevent microbial contamination apply. In general, pickles usually end up considerably more acidic than regular canned tomatoes, so the risk of spoilage is lessened. Most recipes for pickled tomatoes rely on unripe green tomatoes, but there are a few tasty relishes that use ripe red tomatoes.

Sweet Green Tomato Pickles

This recipe calls for sliced tomatoes, although small, whole, green cherry tomatoes can also be used. If you want to spice these pickles up, add a few hot chili peppers to the mix. If stored in a cool, dark place, the pickles will keep well for one to two years. Refrigerate after opening.

Ingredients

2 qt sliced green tomatoes (about ½ to 1 inch thick)

½ qt sliced onions

½ cup pickling salt

½ lb light brown sugar

3 cups vinegar

½ tsp ground black pepper

2 tsp whole cloves

2 Tbsp celery seed

2 Tbsp mustard seed

Cover the tomato and onion slices with salt and let sit for three to four hours. Use cheesecloth or a fine strainer to squeeze excess moisture from the onions and tomatoes. Combine all ingredients in a large pot. Bring to a boil and simmer for about five minutes. Put tomatoes and liquid into hot sterilized jars filled to about ½ inch from the top. Wipe rims clean and seal with metal lids and rims. Process the filled jars in boiling water for about ten minutes. Makes six to eight pint jars.

Dill Green Tomato Pickles

Small unripe cherry or grape tomatoes or sliced or quartered pieces of larger green tomatoes can be used for this recipe. Dill is another one of those tomato-compatible spices that is easy to grow in a pot on the back porch. The red peppers in this recipe are both tasty and make the completed jars colorful.

Ingredients

6 cups small whole or sliced or quartered green tomatoes

1 onion sliced

¼ cup pickling salt

2 sweet red peppers, seeded and sliced

¼ lemon, thinly sliced

6 cloves garlic

2 qt water

1 tsp peppercorns

½ tsp celery seeds

1 Tbsp ground mustard

1 ½ cups cider vinegar

4 tsp fresh dill

Add salt to the green tomatoes and onions and let sit in a cool spot for ten hours. This removes some of the moisture from the vegetables before pickling. Combine all ingredients with the onions and tomatoes and bring to a boil. Boil slowly for 30 minutes. Pack in pint jars. Process the pint jars in boiling water for about ten minutes. Makes four to five pints.

Red Tomato Relish

Sweet relish is another great option for preserving and using an abundant tomato crop in the winter. This relish can be used in tuna, egg, or chicken salad; with hot dogs and hamburgers; and also to spice up lamb or pork dishes.

Ingredients

8 cups chopped red tomatoes

3 sweet Vidalia onions

1 green pepper

2 pears

3 cups sugar

1 cup cider vinegar

2 tbsp salt

1 cinnamon stick

1 tsp mustard seed

1 tsp black peppercorns

½ tsp cloves

½ tsp allspice

1 small piece dried ginger

Peel the tomatoes and peaches by lightly scoring the end and dropping in boiling water for a few minutes. Rinse with cool water. Chop tomatoes and press through a sieve to reserve the tomato fluid. You can use this later to adjust the consistency of the relish. Finely chop all vegetables. A food processor is fine for this recipe, but stop the food processor before you get to the pureed stage. Combine the spices into a cheesecloth bag for boiling with the vegetables. Add all ingredients to a large pot and boil for about 30 minutes. If the consistency is too thick for your taste, add some of the tomato fluid back to adjust. Add to clean hot jars. This should make about four to five pints.

CASE STUDY: COOKING WITH TOMATOES

Nicholas Walker, Certified Culinarian
Banquet Chef, InterContinental
Hotel Buckhead
Atlanta, Georgia

A chef talks about cooking with tomatoes and shares his favorite tomato recipes.

Tomatoes are the perfect medium of creativity when it comes to cooking. I guess the hardest thing is to decide what to do with the perfect tomato. Do you eat it raw with some nice sea salt and cracked pepper, or do you make a savory sauce? The good news and the bad news is that given the diversity in the types of tomatoes and the creativity of the chef, the possibilities are endless. "Learn your tomato" is probably the best advice I can give. For example, beefsteak tomatoes are great for slicing, while plum tomatoes are best for sauces.

The relatively high acidity levels can sometimes make cooking with tomatoes a bit tricky. In addition, acid content can vary among different types of tomatoes. There are differences between cooked and fresh tomatoes, differences among varieties of tomatoes, and differences based on the ripeness of the tomato. I learned this the hard way at the beginning of my career. As a young chef, I was making a pasta sauce that was creamed with artichokes and tomatoes. While the recipe called for stewed tomatoes, I thought I would modify it to use fresh tomatoes.

The fresh tomatoes that I used turned the cream into a broken mess of milksolids that was nasty-looking, to say the least. I learned that sometimes recipes are written the way they are for a reason. With respect to tomato varieties, I love all tomatoes regardless of color, size, or variety. I like using different varieties for different applications. I find plum tomatoes great for sauces and jams, and I use the heirloom varieties for different salads, relishes, and salsas. My favorite type to eat fresh is the little sun-gold-yellow cherry tomato. They are just like nature's little candies.

I stay away from tomatoes in the winter unless we jar or can them. I know that in the winter they are available from other geographies, but by the time they reach us, they are mealy and under-ripened. Also, if they are refrigerated, it changes the taste and texture.

The following are two of my favorite tomato-based recipes:

Smoked Tomato Jam

Ingredients:

> 4 cups diced smoked Roma tomatoes with skins and seeds removed
> 1 Tbsp garlic, minced
> 1 shallot, minced
> ¼ lb smoked bacon, diced small
> 1 Tbsp red wine vinegar
> 1 Tbsp granulated sugar
> Salt and black pepper

To smoke the tomatoes, I like to use the grill and use hickory chips to flavor. Cut the tomatoes in half and place on the grill; allow to smoke for about 30 minutes.

To prepare jam:

Render bacon in saucepan. When bacon becomes crispy, remove the fat and add the rest of the ingredients. Cook for 45 minutes until jam consistency is reached. Adjust seasoning to taste.

Tomato and Brie Tart with Caramelized Onions
(With this recipe, you can use store-bought puff pastry.)

> 4 Roma tomatoes, sliced ¼-inch thick

½ Tbsp olive oil
1 pinch sea salt
Fresh-cracked black pepper
1 sprig fresh thyme, leaves removed
2 cloves garlic, minced
(Toss sliced tomatoes in above ingredients and set aside.)
2 yellow onions, julienned
2 Tbsp butter
1 bay leaf
1 sprig thyme
Salt and pepper

Melt butter. Add onions, bay, and thyme. Cook low and slow for about two hours. Adjust seasoning to taste. Remove thyme and bay leaf and set aside.

For cheese:

4 strips brie cheese (cut from brie wheel)

For pastry:

Bake pastry at 375 degrees Fahrenheit for 15 minutes. Cut into desired shape. I like to cut the sheet into triangles.

To assemble tart:

Spread caramelized onions onto the pastry triangles. Place tomatoes in over lapping pattern on top of the onions. Next place one strip of cheese on top of tomatoes. Bake in oven for 12 minutes at 350 degrees Fahrenheit.

I like to serve this with a salad of arugula and frisée dressed with pesto.

Conclusion:
Ten Tips for Great Tomatoes

It is important to remember: Everyone has a different garden environment with respect to soil, climate, and local pests. Consequently, any information you read must be taken as guidance rather than as rules. The most successful gardener is also an experimentalist who tries a variety of options in the garden and finds the ones that work best for his or her own local environment. Having said this, there are a few general maxims that probably apply to most everyone's garden situation, which include:

1. Prepare soil early, ideally in the fall and plant a cover crop.

2. Have a compost pile and add a lot of organic matter.

3. Plant a diverse group of varieties and cultivars.

4. Plant transplants deep.

5. Mulch to reduce weeds and manage moisture loss.

6. Make sure plants get enough light.

7. Use a drip irrigation system to water.

8. Watch carefully to catch disease or pests early.

9. Protect from local wildlife with fencing.

10. Be creative and resourceful in using and enjoying your harvest.

If you are about to embark on a tomato garden for the first time, then this deep dig into tomato gardening should have given you all you need to know to ensure a great first harvest. If you are a veteran grower, you likely hit upon some twist or tip you might not have otherwise known about or tried before.

It is expected that you can leverage much of this information for improving your total garden soil and increasing your success in growing other garden vegetables.

Appendix A:
Information and Resources

Seed Suppliers

Burpee: (**www.burpee.com**) The largest and potentially oldest seed company in the United States. It was founded and is still based in Pennsylvania. It has an online- and catalog-based business, and also sells seed through retail outlets.

Victory Seed Company: (**www.victoryseeds.com**) An online and ex-catalog business based in Oregon that specializes in rare and heirloom vegetable, herb, and flower seeds.

Gary Ibsen's Tomato Fest: (**www.tomatofest.com**) A Web site focused on heirloom tomato seeds, with more than 600 different heirloom varieties available. The company is based in California. All seeds sourced here are certified organic.

The Seed Savers Exchange: (**www.seedsavers.org**) A non-profit organization based in Iowa and dedicated to saving and sharing heirloom vegetable and flower seeds.

Southern Exposure Seed Exchange: (**www.southernexposure. com**) This seed source is a worker-owned cooperative based in Virginia, near the home of Thomas Jefferson. They specialize in heirloom and other open-pollinated varieties of seeds and grow more than 40 percent of their seeds themselves.

Baker Creek Heirloom Seeds: (**http://rareseeds.com**) A company based in the Ozarks of southern Missouri that specializes in heirloom seeds of a variety of vegetables including tomatoes. An online store is available plus retail stores in Mansfield, Missouri, and Petaluma, California.

Marianna's Heirloom Seeds: (**www.mariseeds.com**) A company that specializes in heirloom and Italian tomato, eggplant, and pepper seeds, and many heirloom transplants. They have an online catalog as well as a farm store in Dickson, Tennessee, that is open on many spring weekends.

Tomato Growers Supply Company: (**www.tomatogrowers.com**) A company based in Florida that specializes in tomato and pepper seeds. They offer more than 500 varieties of pepper and tomato seeds of both hybrid and heirloom types.

Selected Plants: (**www.selectedplants.com**) A small company based in Alabama specializing in shipping heirloom tomato plants to home and small farm gardeners. This source can provide tomato transplants of roughly 200 heirloom varieties.

Sand Hill Preservation Center: (**www.sandhillpreservation.com**) A family seed and poultry company with a good selection of heirloom tomato varieties. The focus of this organization is organic and sustainable gardening.

Totally Tomatoes: (**www.totallytomato.com**) An online and catalog seed supplier based in Wisconsin that specializes in tomatoes, peppers, and growing supplies.

Tomato seeds can also be purchased at local nurseries and gardening stores or large discount or home improvement stores. Varieties may be somewhat limited at these stores, but they are a good source for last-minute purchases.

Useful Web Sites

National Climatic Data Center: (**http://cdo.ncdc.noaa.gov/cgi-bin/climatenormals/climatenormals.pl**) Very comprehensive data on past climate patterns for North America. In particular, this is an excellent site for data on average last spring and average first fall frost dates across the United States.

Mother Earth News: (**www.motherearthnews.com**) A classic publication, and now Web site, with a focus on organic and local gardening issues. The site includes good information on weather data as well.

Farmers' Almanac: (**www.farmersalmanac.com**) Another classic publication that has evolved into a Web site. It includes a variety of farming and gardening advice, such as weather history and forecasts, folklore, and natural garden remedies.

National Gardening Association: (**www.garden.org**) A non-profit organization committed to home gardening, plant education, environmental stewardship, and community development. This is a good Web site for general gardening information on a variety of fruits and vegetables.

Cooperative Extension Service: (**www.extension.org**) A broad information resource on gardens, lawns, animals, and a variety of other topics derived from state university based resources. For a variety of information on tomatoes, go to this site and search "tomatoes."

Vegetable MD Online: (**www.vegetablemdonline.ppath.cornell.edu**) An excellent Web site created by the Cornell University Department of Plant Pathology with information on diagnosing and treating a variety of vegetable diseases.

National Center for Home Food Preservation: (**www.uga.edu/nchfp**) This is an organization of the U.S. Department of Agriculture (USDA) Cooperative Extension Service. It is the definitive resource for the latest instructions for the safe, home preservation of fruits, vegetables, and meats.

There is also an increasing number of gardening Web sites that sponsor forums with insight and information from the gardening community. On these forums, it is possible to find gardeners in every area of the country who will respond to specific questions on local issues, challenges, and opportunities. The following have specific sections on tomatoes:

GardenWeb: The Internet's Garden Community: **www.gardenweb.com**

Garden Forums: **www.gardenforums.com**

The Helpful Gardener: **www.helpfulgardener.com**

Appendix B:
Suggested Reading

The Tomato in America: Early History, Culture and Cookery, Andrew F. Smith. 1994

American Tomato, The Complete Guide to Growing and Using Tomatoes, Robert Hendrickson, 2005

The No-work Garden Book, Ruth Stout and Richard Clemence, 1971

Square Foot Gardening, A New Way to Garden in Less Space with Less Work, Mel Bartholomew, 2005

Giant Tomatoes, Giant Yield, Giant Weights, Marvin H. Meisner, 2007

100 Heirloom Tomatoes for the American Garden, Carolyn J. Male, 1999

The Great Tomato Book, Gary Ibsen, 1999

The Ball Blue Book Guide to Preserving, Jarden Home Brands, 2009

Putting Food By, Janet Greene, Ruth Hertzberg, Beatrice Vaughan, 1988

Appendix C:
State Extension Services

The Cooperative Extension Service is a nationwide nonprofit educational network that provides, among other things, gardening and agricultural information and advice for commercial and home growers on a local basis. Every state in the United States has at least a state office associated with a public state university, and many states have multiple county and local offices in addition to the state office.

State Cooperative Extension Services and Partner Universities

Alabama	Auburn University	**www.aces.edu**
	Alabama A&M	
Alaska	University of Alaska	**www.uaf.edu/ces**
Arizona	University of Arizona	**http://extension.arizona. edu**
Arkansas	University of Arkansas	**www.uaex.edu**
California	University of California	**http://ucanr.org**
Colorado	Colorado State University	**www.ext.colostate.edu**
Connecticut	University of Connecticut	**www.extension.uconn.edu**
Delaware	University of Delaware	**http://ag.udel.edu/ extension**
Florida	University of Florida	**http://solutionsforyourlife. ufl.edu**
Georgia	University of Georgia	**www.caes.uga.edu**
Hawaii	University of Hawaii	**www.ctahr.hawaii.edu**
Idaho	University of Idaho	**www.extension.uidaho. edu**
Illinois	University of Illinois	**http://web.extension.uiuc. edu**
Indiana	Purdue University	**www.ag.purdue.edu**
Iowa	Iowa State University	**www.extension.iastate. edu**
Kansas	Kansas State University	**www.ksre.ksu.edu**
Kentucky	University of Kentucky	**http://ces.ca.uky.edu/ces**
Louisiana	Louisiana State University	**www.lsuagcenter.com**
Maine	University of Maine	**www.extension.umaine. edu**
Maryland	University of Maryland	**http://extension.umd.edu**

Massachusetts	University of Massachusetts	www.umassextension.org
Michigan	Michigan State University	www.msue.msu.edu
Minnesota	University of Minnesota	www.extension.umn.edu
Mississippi	Mississippi State	http://msucares.com
Missouri	University of Missouri	http://extension.missouri.edu
Montana	University of Montana	http://extn.msu.montana.edu
Nebraska	University of Nebraska	www.extension.unl.edu
Nevada	University of Nevada	www.unce.unr.edu
New Hampshire	University of New Hampshire	http://extension.unh.edu
New Jersey	Rutgers University	http://njaes.rutgers.edu
New Mexico	New Mexico State	http://aces.nmsu.edu
New York	Cornell University	http://cce.cornell.edu
North Carolina	North Carolina A&T	www.ag.ncat.edu/extension
North Dakota	North Dakota State	www.ag.ndsu.edu/extension
Ohio	Ohio State University	http://extension.osu.edu
Oklahoma	Oklahoma State University	http://countyext2.okstate.edu
Oregon	Oregon State University	http://extension.oregonstate.edu
Pennsylvania	Penn State University	http://extension.psu.edu
Rhode Island	University of Rhode Island	www.uri.edu/ce
South Carolina	Clemson University	www.clemson.edu/extension'
South Dakota	South Dakota State	http://sdces.sdstate.edu
Tennessee	University of Tennessee	www.utextension.utk.edu
Texas	Texas A&M	http://texasextension.tamu.edu

Utah	Utah State University	**http://extension.usu.edu**
Vermont	University of Vermont	**www.uvm.edu/extension**
Virginia	Virginia Tech	**www.ext.vt.edu**
	Virginia State University	
Washington	Washington State	**http://ext.wsu.edu**
West Virginia	West Virginia University	**www.wvu.edu/~exten**
Wisconsin	University of Wisconsin	**www.uwex.edu/ces**
Wyoming	University of Wyoming	**http://ces.uwyo.edu**

Appendix D:

Garden Log

Keeping track of your gardening experience is a great way to clearly understand what works (and what does not) for your particular climate and location. You can also use your experience to improve your harvest in future years. Your garden log can be as detailed or as general as you like. It can include just the basics, such as planting times and harvest times, or can be extensive and include details on fertilizing, watering, pruning, and local temperatures. It is also helpful to include general comments about pests or diseases that were a problem and remedies that worked for you. The following is a general format to get you started on tracking your garden's progress:

TARGET DATES

PLANTS	Variety	Date Seeds Planted Inside	Date Seeds Planted Outside	Transplants Planted Outside	First Harvest
Tomatoes	Early Girl				
	Better Boy				
	Brandywine				
Peppers					
Squash					
Eggplant					
Cucumbers					
Okra					
Lettuce					
Sugar Snaps					
Watermelon					
Beans					

ACTUAL DATES

PLANTS	Variety	Date Seeds Planted Inside	Date Seeds Planted Outside	Transplants Planted Outside	First Harvest
Tomatoes	Early Girl				
	Better Boy				
	Brandywine				
Peppers					
Squash					
Eggplant					
Cucumbers					
Okra					
Lettuce					
Sugar Snaps					
Watermelon					
Beans					

Glossary of Terms

Annual — A plant that completes its entire life cycle within one year.

Bicotyledon — Plant that germinates from a seed that initially produces two cotyledons or seed leafs.

Blight — A rapid and often complete browning of plant foliage that most often results from a pathogenic organism.

Botany — The scientific study of plant anatomy, physiology, classification, and economic significance.

Cotyledon — A leaf of the embryo of a seed, which upon germination generally emerges, enlarges, and becomes green. This is often called a seed leaf and is different in appearance and origin from true plant leaves.

Cultivar — A variety of a plant that is developed by intentional breeding. The word "variety" is used to refer to a type of plant that results from accidental breeding.

Cutworms — The larvae of a species of moth that grow just beneath the surface of the soil and feed on young plant stems, often killing the entire plant.

Damping off — The wilting or dying of seedlings that is caused by a fungus-based disease and often results from over watering.

Decumbent — A term that describes a growth habit of a plant that lies along the ground.

Dessicant — A substance that has a high affinity for water and will promote drying of the atmosphere around it.

Determinate — A category of tomato plants that grow to a specific height. Determinates produce and ripen all their fruit over a couple of weeks. These are often referred to as "bush" varieties.

Drip irrigation — Using a hose or tube with small perforations to deliver water to the base of plants in a slow, controlled fashion and to promote deep, thorough watering without erosion.

Extension service — In the agricultural context, this is a state- or county-based government program, usually linked to a university, that provides education, information, and support resources to local farmers and gardeners.

Flavonoids — A class of plant metabolites that, in many cases, function as pigments or as deterrents to insect or bacterial attack of the plant or fruit.

Hardening off — The process of gradually exposing seedlings to direct sunlight, wind, and cooler temperatures to acclimate them before they are planted in the garden.

Heirloom tomato — An open pollinated tomato variety that has been in circulation for more than 50 years.

Hybrid — A plant produced from a cross between two plants with different genetic constituents. Hybrids from crosses between crop varieties are often stronger and produce better yields than the original stock.

Indeterminate — A category of tomato plants that do have a limited height but continue to grow and produce fruit until killed by disease or frost.

Larva — The second stage of development in the life cycle of what will become an adult moth. The larva phase is when the insect typically does the most damage to tomato plants. The plural for this word is larvae.

Legume — Plants in the pea family that are distinctive in that they have symbiotic bacteria in nodules on their roots, which give them the capability to fix nitrogen from the atmosphere into the plant.

Locules — The cavities or chambers within a tomato fruit that contain the seeds surrounded by a gelatinous substance.

Lycopene — The chemical found in tomatoes that is responsible for the red color. It is an anti-oxidant whose function is to protect the tomato from the environment and is also thought to be responsible for some of the health benefits of the tomato.

Mulch — A covering of inorganic or organic materials placed over the soil to help control soil temperature, moisture, and weed growth.

Nematodes — Microscopic, worm-like organisms found in soil and water. The root knot nematode is parasitic to tomato plants and a cause of plant disease.

Open pollination — Pollination by insects, birds, wind, or other natural mechanisms. Under open pollination conditions, plants can self-pollinate or can naturally cross-pollinate.

Ovary — The female organ of a plant flower that generally consists of the ovules, which will develop into seeds, and the carpel, which surrounds the ovules.

Perennial — A plant that survives to repeat its reproductive and growing season for at least three years.

Perlite — A natural volcanic rock that when superheated forms small, light, white particles that look and feel like Styrofoam and is used to reduce soil compaction.

pH — An acronym that comes from the potential of hydrogen and is a measure of the acidity or alkalinity of a solution

or medium. It ranges from 0 to 14, with numbers below 7 specified as acidic, numbers above 7 specified as alkaline, and 7 defined as neutral.

Pupa — The third phase in the lifecycle of what will become an adult moth. The larva transforms into a pupa, which then evolve into moths. (The plural is pupae.)

Self-pollination — The transfer of pollen from the male organ of a flower to the female organ of the same flower or to different flowers on the same plant. It can also refer to transfer of pollen from one plant to a genetically identical plant.

Semi-determinates — A relatively small group of tomatoes that have some of the characteristics of determinates, bushy shorter stature, and some of the characteristics of indeterminates, an extended fruit-producing season.

Soil amendment — A material added to the soil to improve its physical structure that will improve characteristics, including such things as permeability, water retention, and drainage.

Stamen — The male organ of a plant flower and the source of the plant pollen. The stamen usually consists of a filament or stalk and the pollen-producing anther at its tip. Flowers often have multiple stamens.

Suckers — Side shoots of a tomato plant that form in the elbow between the main stalk and an existing leaf branch. If left untouched, suckers will develop into new branches.

Taproot — The main tapered, vertically growing root that is often thicker than the other more horizontal lateral roots.

Vascular system — The transport system of the plant that provides for the movement of water, minerals, and photosynthetic products throughout the plant.

Vermiculite — A natural clay-type mineral that, when superheated, forms small, white, lightweight particles that can improve soil structure. The water that the vermiculite contains naturally is superheated, expands, and "pops" open the structure. Superheating water means heating it in conditions that cause it to turn to steam at higher temperatures than the boiling point.

Bibliography

Abdul-Baki, Aref A. and Teasdale, John R., "Sustainable Production of Fresh-Market Tomatoes and Other Vegetables with Cover Crop Mulches," USDA Farmers Bulletin Number 2280, October 2007

Almasoum, A. A., "Effect of Planting Depth on Growth and Productivity of Tomatoes Using Drip Irrigation with Semi Saline Water," III International Symposium on Irrigation of Horticultural Crops

Bai, Yuling and Lindhout, Pim, "Domestication and Breeding of Tomatoes: What have We Gained and What Can We Gain in the Future?" *Annals of Botany*, August 2007, **http://aob.oxfordjournals.org/cgi/content/full/100/5/1085**

Bartholomew, Mel, *Square Foot Gardening, A New Way to Garden in Less Space with Less Work*, 2005

Bennett, Pamela J., "Growing Cucumbers, Peppers, Squash And Tomatoes In Containers," Ohio State University Extension Service

Butterfield, Bruce, "The Impact of Home and Community Gardening In America," National Gardening Association, 2009

Caldwell, Brian, et al, Resource Guide for Organic Insect and Disease Management, October 2005, **www.nysaes.cornell.edu/ pp/resourceguide**

Campbell Soup Web site, **www.campbellsoup.com**

Cook, Roberta, Calvin, Linda, "Greenhouse Tomatoes Change the Dynamics of the North American Fresh Tomato Industry," Economic Research Service, **www.USDA.gov**

Cooperative Extension Service, Deer Damage Management, February 2008, **www.extension.org/pages/Deer_Damage_ Management**

Cotner, Sam, "Vegetable Gardening in Containers," Texas Agricultural Extension Service

Cox, Bonnie, "Field Production or Organic Tomatoes, Oregon Tilth," January 2009, **www.extension.org/article/18653**

Cox, Sam, "I Say Tomayto, You Say Tomahto...," December 2000, **www.landscapeimagery.com/tomato.html**

Cunningham, Sally Jean, *Great Garden Companions: A Companion-Planting System for a Beautiful, Chemical-free Vegetable Garden*, 1998

Davis, J.G., Wilson, C.R., Colorado State Extension Service Gardening Series, "Choosing a Soil Amendment," May 2005, **www.ext.colostate.edu/Pubs/Garden/07235.html**

Department of Entomology, Soils and Plant Sciences, Clemson University Web site, **http://hubcap.clemson.edu/~blpprt/index.html**

Elmore, Clyde, et al, Soil Solarization, "A Nonpesticidal Method for Controlling Disease, Nematodes and Weeds," Publication 21377, University of California

Hendrickson, Robert, *American Tomato, The Complete Guide to Growing and Using Tomatoes*, 2005

Jones, Jr., J. Benton, *Tomato Plant Culture: In the Field, Greenhouse, and Home Garden*, 1991

Lamey, H. Arthur and Draper, Martin A., "Plant Disease Management in the Home Garden," PP-469, February 1995

Lamey, H. Arthur and Draper, Martin A., "Disease Management in Home-grown Tomatoes," PP-659, November 1992

Layton, Blake, "Bug Wise," June 2009, Mississippi State University Extension Service

Lucier, Gary, Lin, Biing-Hwan, Allshouse, Jane, Kantor, Linda Scott, "Factors Affecting Tomato Consumption in the United States," Economic Research Service, **www.USDA.gov**

Meisner, Marvin H., *Giant Tomatoes: Giant Yield, Giant Weights*, 2007

Mississippi State University Extension Service, "Staking and Training Tomatoes," Extension Publication 1091, *Garden Tabloid*, January 2005

Mitchell, Ayson E., et al, "Ten-Year Comparison of the Influence of Organic and Conventional Crop Management Practices on the Content of Flavonoids in Tomatoes," May 2007, University of California, Davis

O'Kennedy, Niamh, et al, "Effects of tomato extract on platelet function: a double-blinded crossover study in healthy humans." *American Journal of Clinical Nutrition*, 2006; 84:561-569

Plummer, Charles, "Modeling the US Processing Tomato Industry, Economic Research Service," **www.USDA.gov, Vegetables and Specialties/VGS-279/November 1999**

Reiners, Steven, "Watering Tomatoes Drip by Drip," New York State Agricultural Experimental Station, **www.nysaes.cornell. edu/pubs/ask/irrigation.html**

Relf, Diane and McDaniel, Alan, "Intensive Gardening Methods," Virginia Cooperative Extension, May 2009

Relf, Diane and McDaniel, Alan, "Mulches for the Home Vegetable Garden," Virginia Cooperative Extension, Publication 326-426

Riotte, Louise, *Carrots Love Tomatoes: Secrets of Companion Planting for Successful Gardening*, 1998

Silaste, M.L., et al, "Tomato juice decreases LDL cholesterol levels and increases LDL resistance to oxidation," July 2007, **www.ncbi.nlm.nih.gov/pubmed/17617941**

Smith, Andrew F., *The Tomato in America: Early History, Culture and Cookery*, 1994

Spooner, David, Peralta, Iris, USDA Agricultural Research Service, "History, Origin and Early Cultivation of Tomato," February 2, 2007

Stout, Ruth and Clemence, Richard, *The No-Work Garden Book*, 1971

Texas A&M, San Angelo, **http://sanangelo.tamu.edu/agronomy/tomato/stems.html**

University of California, Davis, Plant Biology Division, **www-plb.ucdavis.edu/labs/rost/tomato/tomhome.html**

University of Illinois Extension Service Web site, **http://urbanext.illinois.edu/gpe/case2/c2facts1.html**

University of Tennessee Agricultural Extension Service, "Commercial Tomato Products," Publication PB 737

USDA, "Complete Guide to Home Canning, Guide 3, Selecting, Preparing, and Canning Tomatoes and Tomato Products"

USDA Agricultural Research Service, USDA. "USDA Releases New Tomatoes With Increased Beta Carotene." November 2, 1998

USDA Nutrition Web site, **www.nal.usda.gov**

Weaver, John E. and Bruner, William E., *Root Development of Vegetable Crops*, McGraw-Hill, 1927

Zitter, T. A., "Bacterial Diseases of Tomatoes," New York State Cooperative Extension, Fact Sheet 735.50, October 1985

Cherie Everhart grew up watching her dad garden and eventually started gardening herself. She earned a Ph.D. in chemistry from the University of North Carolina, and her career was in corporate research and development for several major corporations. She is now retired from corporate research, but continues to garden. Prior to this book, her writing experience has been technical in nature — including a thesis, technical reports, journal articles, and patents. She currently lives and gardens in Alpharetta, Georgia. Her garden is currently about 2,500 square feet, including a variety of berries and vegetables.

Index